Dedication

THE CRIMSON PILL

Kachien Kiyany

Published by Kachien Kiyany, 2024.

While every precaution has been taken in the preparation of this book, the publisher assumes no responsibility for errors or omissions, or for damages resulting from the use of the information contained herein.

THE CRIMSON PILL

First edition. February 26, 2024.

Copyright © 2024 Kachien Kiyany.

ISBN: 979-8224340330

Written by Kachien Kiyany.

Table of Contents

Having diligently engaged in the process of critical analysis and contemplation, I embarked upon a journey of intellectual exploration and discernment. My biggest question was, "what does the bible say about marriage, polygamy and divorce?' this might look like madness. It is not necessarily the work of a literary expert, neither is it the rumblings of a philosopher, nor is it the pondering of a religious guru, but having listened to religious opinions, my elders, peers and my personal explorations I decided to put it into writing. This is to all men.

BY THE WAY

One day, as I walked into a supermarket, there were attendants placing ceramic plates onto the display shelves. One of them as a by the way told the other, "These are the toughest plates in the world".

"*Uongo!*" his colleague retorted. "*Kama ni ukweli si uangushe moja ulipie!*"

The former attendant without hesitation took the plate that was in his hand and threw it to the concrete floor. The noise was deafening but the plate didn't shatter. They didn't know I was watching. The price was a mere one hundred shillings. I hadn't planned on buying the plates but after what I had witnessed I couldn't resist buying them. I actually started with the plate he had dropped onto the floor. I had seen this unbelievable bargain withstand the test.

Ask and it shall be given. I presume God meant answers as well. Are you like me, taught that some things are never to be questioned? Like the opening scene of the animation Smallfoot? Taught that the foundation of all Christian theology is everything taught by those schooled in theology and that whatever a preacher teaches is unquestionable? Taught that questioning some things whether they be theories, or they be methods or they be hypotheses, or they be beliefs amount to questioning God? Have you ever struggled with raising questions after a sermon? Have you ever felt that there is an unspoken boundary beyond which you cannot question or think?

Well. I do believe that the bible is divinely inspired. My problem starts with dogma. The unquestioned theology passed down from generation to generation. Commentaries having a life of their own after the death of the commenter and his generation.

Are we sure that the theologies we hold dear can, like the ceramic plate, hold in one piece even when intentionally dashed? Do we fear questioning what was brought over from Europe as Christianity out of fear that perhaps it will fail? Is the interpretation of scripture a one sided endemically euro-centric affair? Must the gospel carry westernization whenever it goes? Must it be that any non-European view of the gospel be shunned as not properly Christian? Be referred to as heretic or orthodox where even orthodox is accepted given it has roots in Europe?

In engineering, testing is a crucial step to ensure that a product meets the international standards and regulations. The most important type of tests that I have ever seen are known as destructive tests. The item, usually considered a specimen, is subjected to the most extreme force, temperature, energy till either it gives in or the testing machine can exert no further extremity. This always tells how strong the item is. Raising extreme questions is my way of subjecting Christianity to destructive test. And am confident God doesn't mind. He is not scared his answer to the world will fail.

I have come to the conclusion that any country colonized by Europeans but did not accept Christianity is now very developed. Even in Africa. There's something that dies when you define yourself through someone else's culture. If someone convinces you to define yourself through his culture then that person has mentally enslaved not just you but your children, your grandchildren and even beyond your great grandchildren. What is indigenous to you will always have a footnote of 'inferior' under such mentality.

Is it thus surprising that whoever wants to transform Africa so that Africa answers its own needs using its own solutions, implemented by sons and daughters of Africa so that Africa stands on its own finds he must fight Christianity? From Nyerere, to Samora Machel, to Mandela name any great African leader who didn't find Christianity a hindrance. Name any who didn't find church dogma something that locks Africans into dreaming about the west as if that is a civilization that is next to heaven. Who audited the theology that came with the white man? Who sieved it so that it doesn't make us slaves of Europe? Who analyzed how their consensus was reached at and whether it fits Africa? Who analyzed whether their consensus was applicable eternally or was only relevant in that generation?

Is everything African sin? Is there any godly handwriting evident in our cultures even before the missionaries came? Might it be that in the dogma lies the searing iron that brands the mentality that white man does all the thinking for us? Culture is the teacher of pride in self. Culture represents good or bad, perfect or imperfect dogma gained after ancestral trial and error. Pride in self is the nurturer of innovation. There's something that says, "My ancestors did something so can I" without which even capable brains behave like second class thinkers. All cultures which have pride from history are innovative. Just look at our church posters, there used to be a trend of 'main speaker: so and so from Washington DC'.

It now shifted to the internet. Even the hymns we revere, so European. Even the Swahili and African language hymnals are but translation of European hymnals. If you don't count lyrics composed in your midst worthy of being hymns how will you invent computers? Even the white Christmas, the one event that more than any other alienates Africa from Africans right from childhood. Planting dreams of snow and pine trees and how superior it must be to be white. The European trees. Why can't we just beautify a tree that's there in our yard? At home we tried it and it was beautiful. The obsession with a white father Christmas. I have never seen an African Christmas movie devoid of Father Christmas. I even went somewhere and there was an African woman dressed in the red furry costume, donning the expected hat and struggling to keep the fake beard in place! Didn't know whether to call her mother Christmas or him or her or they or them. All are snow and Father Christmas, so foreign. So alien. At least I have been to Europe during Christmas season and I cannot forget how though I was in the most beautiful of countries I just felt the African soil tugging my conscience that this was indeed an alien celebration. Who audited whether these European centered theology was fit for Africa in the long term? Who? Following this trend won't we then in future be folded up into the western diversity thinking?

Thus I now present an analysis of just one aspect, using my undeniably African trained thinking.

I DESPISED MY FATHER, A SON'S STORY

Yeah it's true. I despised him for a long time. For a long time he was the ogre in my story. And yes he had failed me many times but those failings were not the genesis of spite, something else made it harder to forgive him for being human, made it harder for me to see the father in him, to see the man in him. And little did I know that it started way, way back, to when I was a child.

You see, as a third born you open up your eyes to a family that already has a direction. I was born at a point when the boat was already rocking. I became aware at a time when my parents were already fighting. When I was four my father married a second wife. My mother fought it bitterly. The fights grew even as I grew older. I witnessed some of those ugly episodes. That had a profound effect on me.

As a young boy I was big on church. I remember kneeling at the door of the church with my two friends every day praying on our way back from school. It was our ritual. The church taught me what marriage was. That it is monogamy and God hates polygamy. As I grew older I was even taught that salvation requires polygamous men to send away the "Hagars" and their children. Alluding to the bible story about Abraham's children Ishmael and Isaac. And boy did I pray that my father would enter salvation, cast out the Hagar and her children. Fulfill God's plan. I was taught that men were created to naturally only pair up with one woman at a time. I was so absorbed in this belief that I was quite a bit rude to him.

But some cracks appeared in this theory as I grew. First, when I asked my grandpa, a solid born again *tukutendereza* Christian, how he met my grandmother. He told me as a boy in a catechism class the Anglican priest taught them about Isaac and Rebekah. An argument arose in the class. The whole class told the priest God cannot tell who one should marry. He alone stood and said God can. And the priest told him God would reveal to him. So one night in a dream he sees an angel who tells him "here are your wives, that's the first one and the other's the second one". My grandpa told me that he told the angel "I will only take one" to which the angel pointing to one of the ladies, replied "then she will be the one. Note the mark on her eyebrow". That is how one day he met this girl, my grandmother, who was exactly as he saw in the vision.

They were a match made in heaven. Growing up I saw them love each other till they died. Seventeen kids. They were always thinking of each other. She was so respectful to him. For example, even in her old age she still insisted on carrying his shower water to the bathroom. Those who have grown up with piped water showers and bathtubs may not understand shower from a basin. But it was one way in which she showed him respect. One thing still bothered me. If indeed God spoke to him, why would God offer him two wives? Was that really God? Wasn't God supposed to loathe polygamy? Once in a while I would pick up the question from the mental mysteries box, look at it, and not want to answer, return it to the box. It disturbed a lot of my beliefs. So this planted a question in my mind, is it true that polygamy disgusts God?

And then as I grew up and as I would later realize I created a chasm between me and my father. His masculinity was defined to me as the masculinity I should never have and therefore it was necessary to create a barrier to keep me from absorbing his type of a man. Becoming the type of man he was. I didn't know how this affected me till I was in university. He got born again. Yes he did. But he stuck to what I saw was his Hagar much to my disappointment. Here I was thinking that now that he is born again it's time to cut the baggage and stick to his perfect destiny, my mother. And be like my grandfather. I was busy telling God, "Tell him! He is now born again, he now belongs to you." Shock on me.

Going to university was an escape and culture shock. I used the chance to not speak to my dad at all. As a born again Christian I think I was one happy jumpy guy. Having been a boy's boarding school product from primary school it was the first time I was interacting with creatures called girls at close range. Of course my mother and my sisters don't count and because of the family disagreements I didn't interact with my cousins who simultaneously also don't count as girls. You cannot date them.

At some point I went for an evangelistic mission. It was in Seme. In the vicinity of Bondo ka baba. One day we went door to door preaching in one lakeside village. We would go in pairs. On this day we landed into a polygamous home. This is Luo land that is not a surprising thing. The awkwardness of presenting the gospel to a polygamous home. The person I was paired with started talking of how they were off rail from God's plan and of course there's the subtle jabs about polygamy. Something inside me stirred. Something took over me. At the first opportunity I took over. Words were rolling out of my mouth telling them of how Jesus loves them and of how Jesus wants that home to be united. That Jesus wants to bring peace between the wives. And the man opened up and spoke with tears in his eyes. He never knew that God loves polygamous men. He accepted salvation. He and his wives. I was shocked that I didn't tell him to stick to one wife and chase his Hagars away as I had been taught. As I walked away people questioned my faith. To some, that was heresy. I gathered courage and revisited the question in the box of mysteries. That day one thing was answered. GOD HATES DIVORCE, and that's even for the polygamies. No more labeling people Hagars. That day I dared say God loves people even with polygamy and telling people God does not require them to abandon their wives and children.

I realized, uneasily, reluctantly, that the answer to "does God hate polygamous men?" is simple. No. And I was both uncomfortable and conflicted by this. I still wasn't sure there is heaven for the wives other than the first.

I reached an age where looking for a girl was the in thing. So I stepped into the dating market armed with the typo of my grandfather. Yeah, in my mind I just had to be like him. That I will meet the first one, revealed in a vision, and that will be it. I got no revelation other than the curves, the smiles, the perfumes and my desire for a woman. The first crush ended in a disastrous rejection. The second crush started but ended in horrible rejection worse than the first. I realized I had something missing and it had to do with my masculinity. With hindsight I can confidently declare that this was a direct result of a masculinity shaped by feminism and defined by feminism. There I was seated at a campus event with my catch, looking back I realize she was way out of my league, then some boys from her class came and casually picked her from my side. Hallelujah, someone help me! That's what was going through my numbed thoughts. To date I can still remember her baffled look at me. Her eyes were saying something that I couldn't interpret. The man I had been trained to be was taught never to stand up to wrongs, so I sat and did nothing! Don't they teach that I should turn the other cheek? Seriously does it mean that if one comes for your wife you give them your daughter as a bonus? Don't they emphasize that when asked for my coat I should surrender my shirt as well? But it crushed me. Fela Kuti put it best in his hit Gentleman

You day you go your way
The Jah Jah way
Somebody come bring
Original trouble
You no talk, you no act
You say you be gentleman
You go suffer
You go tire
You go pwench

These teachings of Jesus seemed applicable for something else, misplaced, not meant for all situations. I soon walked out so that I do not cry there out of pitying myself just to meet my first crush at the door who noticed I was going through something. And she sat a bit with me in the lobby as I held back my tears. The simp in me allowed it. I was crying not out of sorrow but anger. I walked out because I was uncomfortable with me. Out of that experience, I formulated a question. What is a man? Because a bad experience is a learning point that should never be wasted. What is a man and what was the

Godly manly thing to do at that point? I knew my reaction was faulty. Then I started reading and searching for answers. I still despised my dad.

Two books shaped that phase of my life. Maximized manhood and one by John Eldregde; wild at heart. I learnt a bit of what being a man is, from books! I gathered courage and faced those boys for snatching a girl from my side. I realized that when it comes to being a man you fight for your girl. Turning the cheek and giving the shirt shouldn't be thought of there. That is for evangelism. Ties in with *How blessed you are when people insult you and persecute you and tell all kinds of vicious lies about you because you follow me! Rejoice, be glad, because your reward in heaven is great — they persecuted the prophets before you in the same way* (CJB). Your family is neither your cheek nor your shirt. It felt good, though belated. I believe God expects a man to protect his woman. I had failed her. I had failed me. But at least I got something from the ashes, a lesson from the scar. I think I improved so much because that year I was put in charge of organizing men's dinner for the Christian union. With hindsight, I now realize, I had morphed from something into the best man feminism can make. A virtuous stronger simp. Still, I despised my dad.

That's the man who entered the dating market. I started out as a man who lets the girl do whatever she wants. I was taught they are infallible delicate jewels. You know, in church they teach masculinity as all about the girl and the kids. I was actually told 'he who finds a wife finds a good thing and obtains favor from the Lord' actually means success starts with getting a wife. I sought for one good thing desperately. Who wouldn't want God's favor? I couldn't wait to start being successful and favored.

At one time I found myself dating two girls and fully comfortable with that. And they knew it. When I was with girl A I would be fully with her. When I was with girl B I was fully with her. And I was enjoying it. But after some months I hated the fact that this looked more like my father and isn't this what made me despise him? And God doesn't allow polygamy, or does he? So I dropped them both. Finally, after many more adventures I got a girl. Married her. Still the best man feminism can make.

They even taught me that if my wife is angry with me God won't hear my prayers. Believe it or not there's a whole teaching on that out there 1 peter 3:7. What they forget is that this verse is just a subset of something Jesus said. Matthew 5:23-24. *So If you are offering your gift at the temple altar and you remember your brother has something against you, leave your gift where it is by the altar, and go make peace with your brother. Then come back and offer your gift.* In short even a woman would have her prayers hindered if her husband is hurting because of her. Very common notion from church that women are perfect angels always being wronged by men. I have come to learn that 1 peter 3:7 does mean women are the bridge between husbands and God.

I trusted the church with teaching me what masculinity is. With hindsight I now realize the picture of a man the church has is Mr. nice guy virtuous simp. With time realities of marriage quickly forced me to introspect. There was a beast inside me whom I had suppressed. I even joined Man enough program. Some wise man said wisdom is the result of seeking wisdom. The question I had added in campus still drove me. What is a man? What are the ingredients of masculinity? And I still remember the 5 pillars of masculinity. Lead sacrificially, Love faithfully, leave a legacy, and take initiative, live responsibly. Good values. Only that there is a tint of feminism lurking somewhere in the details. For example. Leading should never be focused on sacrificing even though sacrificing is part of leading. There's vision casting, enforcing discipline, being self-led before leading others before there is sacrificing. When a lion comes to the herd of buffaloes the bulls in facing the lion are not offering themselves to be eaten but they are exposing themselves to danger to keep the cows and the calves safe. Of course over time I have seen so many versions of the pillars of manhood than I can count.

And then, as the years wore on, Christians whom I knew to be based, grounded in faith, started divorcing. Friends whom I thought were romances made in heaven. It was like a flu. Even people who had gone into training to be better men. Then I looked around and I realized that in my parents' generation they sorted the family trouble in two ways. Some accepted the second and the nth wives. Some went for divorce. My dad, in tune with our traditions, used to tell me stories of days gone together with Luo customs. And one thing he said is that divorces were there but very few. Then I looked around and realized that of the women who stayed and accepted they were in a polygamy, many lived to ripe old age. Not all, but many. Not extremely happy. But happy. Some even made peace with their co-wives. Of those who swallowed the feminist ideals many had issues. They became successful career-wise but the loneliness and the clear need to prove right the lyrics *"as long as I know how to love I know am still alive,... I will survive"*, they had issues. Majority of the men I saw seemed to move on and many made new homes.

This forced me to ask myself, which solution God would prefer, the divorce or polygamy? Does God hate polygamy the way he does divorce? What is the basis of this unquestioned Christian law that we Christians ensured is even enshrined in the Marriage Act 2014? The question opened a Pandora's Box. Why does God in the old testament come across as based, in touch with reality, a God who understands men and women and knows he didn't create them same yet in the new testament as God who is a feminist who is just all about heaven? From the preacher's interpretations on many matters especially on matters of men, women and marriage it sounded like the man God created in the Old Testament is different from the man born again preached from the New Testament. And there is the question of when the bible says "if anyone is in Christ the old is gone the new has come" does it mean my biology as a man changes as soon as I become saved? If it doesn't what then is the new creation? The old question Nicodemus asked Jesus about going back to the womb explains it. It isn't a biological change, it's spiritual. This made me realize that the first foundation of masculinity is reality. A firm grasp of reality is what separates a man from an effeminate man. God made men with a mind that sieves out delusion. Logic is about reality!

Then a verse I had ignored floated to the top of my thoughts. 1 Timothy 3:2a - a bishop must be blameless, the husband of but one wife. This verse *ilinichokoza*, quite literally it red pilled me. If you tell someone "go to the shop and only buy the soap written 'menengai'" does that in any way suggest there is only 'menengai' on the shelf? Quite the opposite. If you specify that polygamists should not be bishops then it means polygamy is not outlawed! So I set off to find out more. I consulted professor google. Where did monogamy enter the church as a law? Something told me to check Roman belief in marriage. Bingo! Found it!

Did you know that by law the Romans were only allowed one wife? It did not come from the church, it came to the church. Even Jews who bought citizenship before Rome became Christian were required to abandon their other wives. This was the exact thing I was taught. It wasn't bible but Roman culture! Christian history, after all, is written in Roman ink! So all these teachings where Christ has men as 2nd class citizens of heaven, powerless, subdued, no initiative because if you anger your wife God won't hear you, all of that teaching, feminism defined masculinity, full of something unrealistic and illogical about it. That teaching that seems to suggest that the only way a man can be his own man is if he is like Paul, celibate. MGTOW, men going their own way. That Jesus came and left a trap and a prison for men called Christian marriage.

It suddenly explained why Christian marriage became the new leading cause of divorce in Africa. They call it the door that as many are trying to get in as are trying to get out. A door to a trap of sorts. Seriously, someone needs to do research. A comparison between divorce rates in traditional non-western Christian influenced societies versus western Christian influenced societies. Numbers don't lie. The church is supposed to produce strong marriages. On this front, it has failed. Our traditional marriage setup was stronger. Teenage pregnancies came with the church. If the church accepted Roman tradition, why didn't it accept to borrow what the bible accepts in the African tradition?

At this point I realized that I despised my father based on a misguided teaching. For the first time in decades I spoke to him as my father. For the first time in decades we had a conversation. For the first time. I called my mother and thanked her for not divorcing because divorce is like a hereditary disease. It follows children. It plants a virus of bitterness. It is violence. No wonder God hates it. So I write this, first to you who like me was taught that polygamy is unholy and led you to hate your mother or father. Here is a reason to ask for forgiveness. Then I also address you who for some reason is now in polygamy. God loves you. God loves your wives, yes, your wives. I may be no preacher, no marriage counsellor, but, this i know, God is there to bring peace, unity and understanding in your home. Let no one tell you that to be accepted by God you have to throw them out. That is divorce. God hates divorce. I am writing to you lady considering divorce. There's a high likelihood it won't give you peace. You can try the old way, let him get another one. You will have him, your children will grow under the shelter, provision and protection of their father and in old age you won't be alone. And if you change your heart about him he still is yours, shared but yours.

The number of people I carried in my heart because of this teaching is untold. Asking for forgiveness from my father's pastor was the highlight for me. Was quite humbling. I had counted the pastor as the enemy of progress. Admitting that he was not wrong in not insisting my father throw out the other wife was a moment. The freedom I felt after that was unquantifiable. How many people are you carrying in your heart because the church convinced you that God loathes polygamy?

FEATHERLESS BIPED

The story goes that Plato told his students that mankind is just a featherless biped. On hearing this his rival, a cynic, delivered a plucked chicken to Plato's school. Called it Plato's man.

Well, is this just a worldly view, that man is basically an animal? Certainly not. Ecclesiastes 3:18-21

I said to myself regarding the sons of men, "God is surely testing them in order for them to see that [by themselves, without God] they are [only] animals." For the [earthly] fate of the sons of men and the fate of animals is the same. As one dies, so dies the other; indeed, they all have the same breath and there is no preeminence or advantage for man [in and of himself] over an animal, for all is vanity. All go to the same place. All came from the dust and all return to the dust. Who knows if the spirit of man ascends upward and the spirit of the animal descends downward to the earth? - AMP[1]

Here Solomon, before the days of Plato, reminds us that we are animals. Indeed we are just animals whose biggest muscle is the brain. This gives human beings advanced cognitive abilities, along with ability to understand the past as well as forecast the future and create. It gives us our ability to develop clear social structures, command structures, laws and traditions.

We have eyes, just like other animals. We have mouths and stomachs and blood doing the same thing that the blood of other animals do. Diseases cross from other animals to the animals called man and vice versa. Just the other day minks

---

1. http://www.biblegateway.com/
passage/?search=Ecclesiastes3:18-21&version=AMP

were being exterminated because apparently they could catch COVID 19 and pass it back to man. We even use animal parts on human beings. We use chicken intestines to stitch up wounds. We use pig insulin as substitute for human insulin. Other animals have other muscles. Lions run and are powerful. Eagles fly. Tortoises have shells. Elephants have tusks and trunks with 40,000 muscles. Man has a powerful brain. Some animals even exhibit useful brains. I have seen research where a chimp was playing a video game. Octopuses are known to manipulate traps. Elephants are known to remember routes to water and food even after 40 years. Woe unto you if you built a house on such a route. You will see what some Kenyans see when the herds of elephants decide to go to their old watering hole. Chimps are known to use some sort of medicinal leaves. Some animals are known to use tools.

Think of circus animals. Semblance of memory and thought? I have even seen a mother chimp mourning its newborn thinking it is dead only for the vets to revive the chimp-let. The mother chimp reaction to seeing its baby lift its arm was heartwarming, exactly like a human mother would do. We humans even do many studies on animals to understand human beings. Case in point is the Pavlov's dogs experiment about instinct or the Gordon Stephenson real experiment with rhesus monkeys that resembles the famous hypothetical 5 monkeys in a cage who would be punished for trying to reach bananas. As such we are animals with brains and a mandate to subdue from God. I am an amateur in biology at best but these things I have seen.

As such it is interesting to ask, is polygamy a product of a God's creative ability or the product of patriarchy and men's greed? Is it a human invention or is it the result of what is embedded in the code of creation? By the way, at this point I must state that all this is based on a firm belief that the bible happened and science just proves it. To me even the big bang is proof of the bible. Because existence is a product of time. Outside time, a dimension we have no ability to start grasping, time being the box to which our greatest imagination is confined, God. You cannot even say 'was God' or 'is God' because 'was' and 'is' are time bound definitions and he created time. Hence the first word of the bible is very apt, "in the beginning". Bang! And things began. The big bang is real. The sudden start of time, of existence, of energy. Scientists even tell us that the earth was a mass of gas and rocks and there was no sun. Eeeh! Sounds like the verses that come after the beginning. The earth was formless and void. Then they say the earth was fully covered in water. You know where else that appears? Chapter 1 of the bible. The spirit of the Lord was hovering over the waters. The bible is accurate. In short, the creator created time. Even his self-given name. Talk of philosophical depth. I AM. I exist. Before time existed, God. Science just exists to prove that and to maximize the box he created called time. I am no religious expert nor physics nor astronomy expert but with what I have, I observe. Indeed God exists, not because I or anyone else believes He exists but because He Is. All we do is acknowledge this fact, recognize his majesty and worship him for it and that to me is faith.

I hear someone shouting why should we care what God thinks, there is EVOLUTION! So let us apply science on this theory that has been dogmatically taught. For cells to exist the DNA must have existed. For DNA to exist there must have been amino acids in a medium where they meet and in such large numbers otherwise they would have to be indestructible. If we were made from indestructible amino acids we would never die. For the amino acids to be so many then producing them would be so easy for nature we would still be seeing sources bubbling with these primordial DNA strands. If they combine so easily then there would at least have been one story of a new unicellular creature discovered in our rubbish dumps which are awash with DNA strands. Like say half banana half pineapple DNA strand. And by the way, can DNA survive without the cell wall. So where did that strand conveniently get a cell wall to ensure its survival? If they miraculously got that complex cell wall that evolved at just the right time to encompass a mass of short DNA strand then how did the cell wall know which other cell to mate with and for new DNA? This is tantamount to assigning intelligence to a group of atoms! How intelligent is that?

The picture below is of a LED, a resistor and a charged capacitor. You can do the same experiment, put them in a tray.

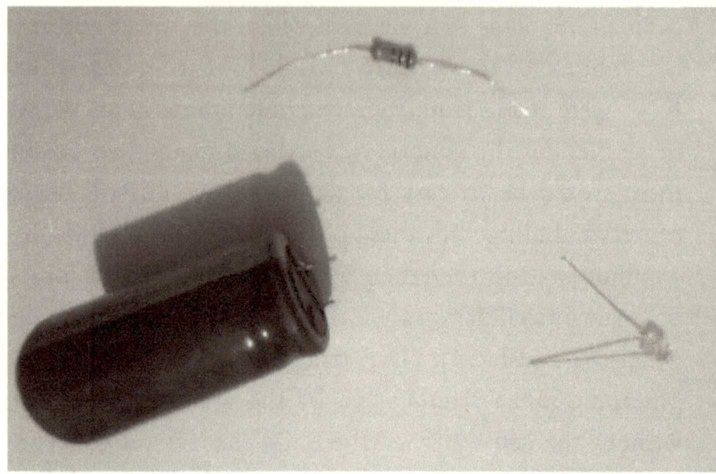

How many millions of years of continuous shaking will it take so that they connect themselves into a circuit? Disclaimer: in this we have skipped the step where the components suddenly appear, creating themselves. Kindly consider that there is only a specific way in which they can connect. If they do manage to do so then how many years will it take them to successfully look for other components and form robots? How many more years before the robots become so advanced they can produce smaller robots within their bodies in internal portable mini fabrication labs? How many millions of years for the robots to evolve such that they consume other robots from which they get energy and components to grow? Won't they need to be intelligent and able to move on their own for them to do this? It is sheer lunacy to believe that atoms and molecules can be intelligent. Evolution never even started! They haughtily say religion is the opiate of the masses. In many ways we have ensured they are right. But they fail to see how evolution theory is the opiate of the educated.

To call the creator intelligent is an understatement that is acceptable because I lack greater words to describe how he awes me with his wisdom. Of his intelligence He says: *Adonai made me as the beginning of his way, the first of his ancient works. I was appointed before the world, before the start, before the earth's beginnings. When I was brought forth, there were no ocean depths, no springs brimming with water. I was brought forth before the hills, before the mountains had settled in place; he had not yet made the earth, the fields, or even the earth's first grains of dust. When he established the heavens, I was there. When he drew the horizon's circle on the deep, when he set the skies above in place, when the fountains of the deep poured forth, when he prescribed boundaries for the sea, so that its water would not transgress his command, when he marked out the foundations of the earth, I was with him as someone he could trust. For me, every day was pure delight, as I played in his presence all the time, playing everywhere on his earth, and delighting to be with humankind. "Therefore, children, listen to me: happy are those who keep my ways. Hear instruction, and grow wise; do not refuse it. How happy the person who listens to me, who watches daily at my gates and waits outside my doors. For he who finds me finds life and obtains the favor of Adonai. But he who misses me harms himself; all who hate me love death." Proverbs 8:22-31 CJB*

Back to what he created. Are the basics of polygamy and monogamy coded in the social interactions of other animals created by the same God? First of all. Males, especially of what I would call the higher animals, mammals, are optimally designed for dispersion of genes. Someone jokingly commented that one man can repopulate an island full of only women while a woman cannot repopulate an island full of only men. Females the opposite. Males are generally gifted with billions of sperms in a lifetime. Active 24 hours 7 days a week, 12 months for years. Requiring the least provocation to disperse them. Whether it's a baboon or a lion or an elephant or a monkey or a porcupine. Some animals are monogamous, like the grey wolf. 3-5% of all mammals are monogamous by nature, 29% of all primate species (Wikipedia). A few are suspects of promiscuousness, like the bonobos and chimpanzees. The bonobos are interesting. They have achieved what feminists have not. The bonobo community is basically Amazonia. The females rule. So. How different biologically is the human male from the other animals? As the late Myles Munroe put it men are not sick for needing lots of sex. They are not demon possessed. Blame the male sex drive on God. He says a man who finds himself needing sex should marry. In my tribe they would say someone whose blood is hot. So men who marry need sex. It's a need, not a diabolic want.

I consider myself lucky to have experienced farm life. If a cow is on heat, that is when it is ripe for impregnation, it attracts bulls. Bulls fight for that chance. Just the way men jostle over women. Many times you as the farmer may desire to improve your stock so you buy semen from established farms and do artificial insemination. In order to succeed it forces farmers to lock their poorer quality bulls up because the bull senses a cow on heat nearby and goes wild. Woe unto you if it breaks loose and you are between it and the cow.

And it even gets more interesting. It is by God's design that the strongest animal is gifted with ability for the most mating. That is core to the survival of any species. Even the jostling for the chance to mate is God made. It cuts across all the animals, doesn't it? The fight to the right. The male status is earned.

Then there's the female cycle. A great proof that whoever created the horse and the cow created human beings. Women naturally are on a cycles, just like other animals. I hear theirs is menstrual while most mammals have estrous. Let's imagine that human beings didn't have big IQ. That they weren't bombarded with sex in all movies and practically have aspects of sex mixed into practically every advertisements. Even sexless things like cooking oil. The way cows and baboons live. Would ladies be trying to outdo men in who can get more game than the other? Another proof that men seek sex more is that even in the most liberal Westernized country, there doesn't seem to be a proliferation of male prostitutes making money from women who want to pay for sex to the same level that female prostitutes virtually are all over. Even in remote villages. In the female prostitutes you get the oldest profession on earth. I have never heard of a male analogous of a brothel. What would we call such, a sistel? I mean brothel is just brother with the 'r' changed to 'l'. So ever seen a sistel? Or men trafficked for sex even with droves of women for decades making their own money and being independent.

So biologically, from observation and comparing with the rest of creation, some men are likely to need more sex than their women will. That's what our forefathers taught. Blame it on God. Not the men. And what does monogamy do? Monogamy seeks to constrain these men to the dwindling sexual appetite of the woman. She is not to blame. They say a woman passes from maiden to mother to matriarch. Somewhere past the maiden stage many rumor that things don't work as before. Life happens but traditionally neither were men to be punished because life happens. Also unlike the single unbelieving woman who may be going for casual sex the married woman in many a tale changes with circumstances. Some men are kept on a diet of tasteless intimacy. There was one short Swahili clip where the man is agitated and complaining of being denied sex by the lady insisting that their son sleeps in their bed. Also another famous meme where the man is told, *"kula ya watu wakubwa, usiguse ya watoto, ukimaliza nifunike"*(eat the adult food, don't touch the children's food, when you are done cover me). The cares of life seems to lower what some women have to offer sexually leaving the man unsatisfied. One does not need to imagine the conflict that arises from these diametrically opposite needs. There are undeniably many women who need and want sex for a few times in a whole month. Similarly there are many men who need and want sex many times more yet are married to these women. She may even want intimacy without sex, yet by the time he gives some intimacy he wants sex. Tough conflict. If a man didn'tneed sex he wouldn't marry. Blame it on God who created this conflict. He is the creator. And that's why I firmly believe he is the one who created polygamy or at least he encouraged it.

FORSAKING ALL OTHERS

Not all men are meant for monogamy. Even Jesus said some men are created eunuchs. Meaning there's a range from men created starting with those who should never marry to those who need and can handle more than one. By God's design. Sex is a need for those not created eunuchs. For some, not you dear angelic man, for some of us it ranks somewhere up there next to food.

The worst legacy of the church under Rome was the culture of treating male libido as a demonic urge, a problem, to be exorcised at every opportunity. Where sex is viewed as the sacrament that exorcised it albeit temporarily. From where I stand they depicted it as a luxury that men should consider living without so as to maintain high standards of holiness. To the Roman root of Christianity, men are supposed to have less sex and to them, achieving celibacy and overcoming the need for sex is holiness. Self mental castration. Unrealistic. In total opposition to The Creator's command in Genesis 1:28 *be fruitful, multiply, fill the earth and subdue it.*

Let me share one example, a hypothesis that is drawn from the experience of some men. It should not be taken as universal occurrence as it has not been scientifically surveyed. The figure below shows a cow and a bull tethered to each other. They move together. Sleep in the same bed. Eat together. You know that song of how they make matching clothes? Have calves who look like them. Because they are tethered to each other the bull can only jump on his cow. If the bull's sexual energy can only be silenced by five cows she has to give it to him like she is five cows because that tether called marriage vow compels him to push all his wildness in her direction. He rides her like she is five cows. For some time. And for some years the cow tries to keep up. The urge in the bull, virility and strength needing action is a need for the bull. Not a want. Not a wish.

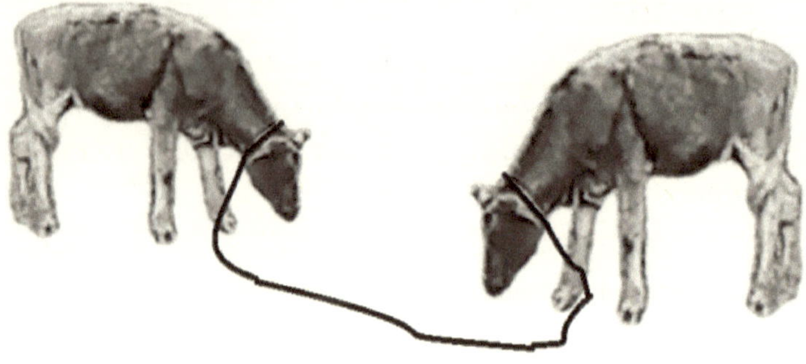

Then somewhere down the road something triggers her. Maybe her biology. And she figures, well, he isn't going anywhere. The tether is strong. It can withstand anything. So she decides she cannot be rode like five cows and the bull's libido is not her problem. He should adopt to her curve in any case. It's his problem. He should rein himself in. He is mandated to have self-control as she has bigger things to handle. So she becomes more like a stake driven into the ground with him tethered to her. Headache here, pain there, am tired, those age old lines become cliche. And like a wooden stake she is unmoved. Some say it is the kids. Maybe. Some say it is the work. May be true. Some say emotional and hormone issues. Am no doctor. Some even claim that the guy lacks bedroom innovation. Well, if that's the case then even if he practices to porn level proficiency and learns Kamasutra she will still eventually get bored. Even those who ate manna finally got bored and yet it was food made in heaven and delivered at their doorstep. Whatever the case she becomes less sensitive to his urges and every other Sunday the preacher goes on the pulpit to chide the men for not being like women. Telling them how God doesn't hear them because their wives are angry. A feminist whip for chastising men. You hear common philosophies like, "*nyumba yenye bwana amekaliwa ndio huendelea*". Literally the house where the man is sat on progresses. Telling the men *vumilia*.

Vumilia. Persevere. A bachelor can take a cold shower and he will be fine. But a married man will come from the cold shower, see his wife and require another cold shower. How many cold showers can one take in the cold of the night?

Telling the young men that their favor starts with getting a wife. Oh yes, you hear preachers speak of the verse that says he who gets a wife gets a good thing. So, lady if you accept you are a thing then that interpretation makes sense and you are infallibly good. But, in case you believe you are not a thing then I propose to you that the thing spoken of is marriage. Marriage is spoken of as the good thing, you are just as wicked and in need of Jesus as any man is. Making women the intermediary between men and their savior as if God is some woke activist or feminist! Even the phrase, "behind every successful man is a woman", has to be checked. Does it mean men who are made for success will fail if they do not marry? Then the catholic church would never have grown. It is fully run by men. Forgetting to tell women that a foolish woman, with her own hands destroys her home yet that's in the bible! So now you have a bull tethered to an insensitive stake that occasionally turns into a cow on heat. In the words of You-tuber @dadvocate it is a slow and painful death for a man when a woman starts treating him like she is doing him favors.

In short, the good sex naturally drops down the list of the many good things she is doing. In reality, the woman, sexually, is now the wooden stake, the vows are the tether and the bull trudges on unhappy but told vumilia because the kids are fine and the food is nice and that's enough exchange, it compensates for the less sex. Don't they say exchange is not robbery?

For a while this holds and then as is normal in life another cow on heat passes by. What do you think will happen? Your guess is as good as mine. Anyone who has been near bulls knows how dangerous it is to stand between a tethered bull and a cow on heat. With time the tether becomes weaker. At some point the bull will break the tether. Even if the bull is normally the most docile.

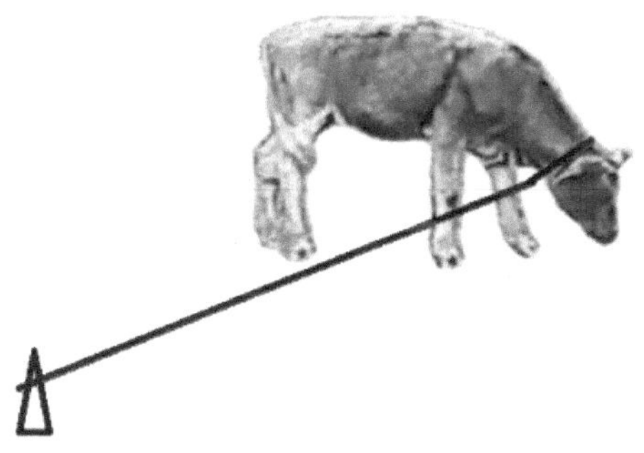

Kindly remember that sexlessness weakens the tether of the vows. Even when a marriage is not consummated after the wedding a divorce is issued no questions asked. Also many men describe the rare sexual rejection as one of the worst humiliation. It is so humiliating that the man may either become violent to the point of forcing it out of his wife, marital rape being a real phenomenon, or a man may even shy from initiating sex this situation thus creates two extremes. It's like being hungry, the cake is yours. You have prepared to eat but you are told you cannot eat because you have to wait for your wife's appetite to come back. So the lady may think he has toned down his "lust", mentally castrated his libido to manageable level matching hers, but in reality it is either piling or being released elsewhere. He cannot be seeing you, a woman, his wife, close proximity, regularly and life goes on as if he is immune, made of stone. Worst case scenario that may mean a guy has learnt to not thirst for sex if that were possible.

I mean, dear pastors, how does saying vows in your presence enable a man to stay monogamous? How? What miracle does the vow bequeath all these people saying them? Or do you say FAITH? Didn't the man after God's heart, David, have faith? Didn't Abraham have faith? Didn't Solomon have faith? Do you want to tell me that God of the Old Testament had more grace for men than in the New Testament? Polygamy is God having grace for the human race. Enforced monogamy is so unrealistic that it has to be propped up by feminism, putting a higher price for the man to pay through divorce processes where everything the man does is deemed duty and everything the woman does is counted as a favor to him. Even giving birth is counted as a favor to the man. Unafrican philosophy. Actually in the Roman traditional marriage environment as recorded in history is so much what I have grown knowing is a Christian standard that it is confusing whether it belonged to the roman or the church. Roman marriage sounds like the theology and practice of church marriage . One and the same thing. Down to the over emphasis on marriage being about property and status.

Even the types of marriage they had. They had *Coemptio* which is what we now call civil marriage. They had an official and five adult witnesses. They had *usus* what is now famous as come we stay. If she lives with you and you sleep with her for a whole year and then after that if she stayed for three more days she was legally your wife. Notice the presence of the number three. How many countries have the idea of somehow married then after a count of three years, three months they become accepted as married? Then they had *confarreatio* exactly what we call Christian or white wedding. Two priests and ten witnesses. Many men stay monogamous because men are wired to keep contracts. That is not faith but it works camouflaged as faith. Even engagement, *sponsalia*, and the fact that the girl has more say than her father is roman freedom. Not bible.

The Romans had safety valves for men for pressure relief, prostitutes and slaves. They were an integral part of roman society. At first due to the Gothic heritage of the prostitutes they had blonde hair. They even regulated it and it was required that all prostitutes dye their hair blonde. They were an integral institution. The west still has this institutions and wherever they go these institutions go. Name one African tribe that had prostitution as an institution. Just one. The church came. The colonizers followed. Prostitution as an institution followed closely. You cannot have monogamy as a law without prostitution. They occupy the same space. Christianity doesn't run brothels but the embedding of roman culture creates a huge customer base for brothels like it did in Rome. If you force everyone to hop on one leg you create a market for crutches. Elephants will need more crutches and millipedes will need a thousand. And to prove this did the Maasai have prostitutes? I know the Luo didn't have a koinange street equivalent. Did the kikuyu have a house where any man enters and pays for sex and as you walk out you meet the next person who is going to pay walking in? Or the Kamba, or the Turkana, or the Ndorobos? These things were in Rome, Greece and China since more than a millennium ago! An oversupply of unmarried women and an undersupply of sex at home plus money makes a messy mix.

At this point I remember a day I was looking for a Kamau on Luthuli Avenue who rewinds transformers because I had a failed one. Someone pointed out a building and told me. "Ask there. He is famous." So I went into the building. What I didn't know is that the building had two wings and I entered the wrong one. This wrong wing was a brothel and here too there was a famous Kamau. Wah! The horrors my innocent eyes saw. Growing up in church I never knew such a world existed. I felt like I was standing outside the walls of new Jerusalem and any time *bel sibuth* would appear and sing *higini gi higini* reminding me am in hell where I would burn forever. By the time I located the Kamau I was being directed to on the third floor, I realized his work was to distribute condoms, not repair transformers. No wonder I was getting funny smiles and offers on my way up the stairs. Before I ran out of the twilight zone building I noticed decent men, clean, looking very normal, cutting deals with twilight girls in broad daylight, in the morning. In the morning! These were the bulk of the customers. Normal everyday men going to work. That urge cannot be silenced by *riswa!* Do not expect faith like Elijah to sort these matters.

Tusijidanganye. Even the bible says the answer to burning with passion, translate to sexual desire, is marry. And there's no verse telling men sex is evil, tone it down. No verse telling men that they have a duty to desire less. Self-control is good, necessary and possible, but everyone has a limit to it. Some people can self-control with one wife some with a few wives. If a man could just give his erection an angry look and the desire goes away the world would be a better place. Once a man marries he knows he is free to want sex. He removes his foot from the brakes. It is like a car on a down slope and on gear free mode. It can propel on gravity alone. In other words when the pastor convinces you dear lady that you can contain that agile virile man till death do you part he is in effect saying that the man won't need to pay a prostitute, won't be pushed to go for one night flings, won't need to involuntarily fast from sex, throttle his libido, because he has you. You are his medicine, miraculously self-replenishing full dose, for burning with passion.

You, his only one, are his medicine whether his prescription from The Creator reads once weekly, twice weekly, 1 x 1, 2 x 1, whatever. Monogamy makes it your duty, I repeat, duty is not do if you feel like, and to joyfully absorb all his sexual need. All. And that is what submission in the bedroom means. Submission elsewhere without this submission is underwhelming submission. Even if he needs it as much as he needs food. If he is created a man of ten times a week, morning and evening, morning and evening... ad libitum then that's what you signed up for. That's the real meaning of him "forsaking all others". It means you are equal to the "all others" combined. You are his all others. The fact that he has a wife his psyche is set to "I can get it when I want it. I need it I get it". If he needs it twenty times a week then that's what you said "I do" to. That is why God created polygamy because he created sexual appetite incompatibility. He himself calls one sex 'weaker'.

As I pointed out,I was raised in a farming environment, and I am reminded of a time when the resident cock was left with about two hens after a series of events(we sequentially stored them in our bellies). The few hens were left in the hell of satisfying the cock's libido. They couldn't even eat in peace without the cock pouncing on them. even the feathers on their backs thinned out from the incessant action. A high libido man with unmatched libido woman will end up with the sex occupying a huge chunk of the relationship yet still as much as that kind of a woman may give more than she can the man still gets less. Don't we know men who are frustrated and irritable because their eve is giving him less? Haven't you heard in an office people comment, "*huyo anatuletea* stress za bibi hapa." While the woman will hate him for being insatiable. This kind of sexual incompatibility is God made and God has a solution for it. So this message is for those who admit they are the weaker, not you strong feminist lady, continue pretending you are strong for the sake of your greed.

This is for those who accept they are 'weaker' which does not mean you are weak. In Luo traditions there was a process called *ywayo*. Literally pulling or grabbing. After the negotiations one would grab his now wife when she is going to collect firewood and carry her to his home. If during the process she escaped and went and touched her mother's waist the groom would be fined. They would ask if you expect your mother in law to come sort issues in your house. As such men always accepted their level of strength and picked a woman weaker than them.

At this point let me use three terms to describe a hypothesis of something that I have seen. Sex too has quality, quantity and satisfaction indices. In my view quantity is defined by how many times it is given. Quality is in my view shown by how many times the giver also needs it. Satisfaction is defined as how beneficial it is to the recipient as well as how he quenches her fire. As I am talking from the man's point of view the man is the recipient. Some say, and I concur, that women are the gatekeepers of sex. So sex is a woman's to give and a man's to ask.

Let's say that because of life, a hypothetical woman, let us call her Ciku, can only joyously need it once a week. Any more than that will be draining her already drained energy. Yet her man was made for a natural frequency of four shots a week. She might actually give the four times but because it takes too much from her and too much of something is poisonous it will be more of do it and get done with it. It becomes work, like going to the office. The man is then just a demanding job. Not a fun giver. She reports to work in bed. She is overworked. The man takes it because he is obliged to take it, the pastor said so. If he doesn't it will cause chaos. So he just goes in to "pour". Her work to give, his work to pour. And I believe it drains love and turns the whole relationship into mechanical duty for both of them. Any man loves to be desired. Loves to feel wanted. There's something magical to men about being wanted. Being given yet not being wanted is just consensual rape. It kills the quality. In turn it lowers satisfaction for the man. It drains reserves of mutual satisfaction. This I believe spills into everything about the family. He is there for the duty. She is there for the duty. How strong is that bond? Below is a hypothetical picture. Yet to be quantitatively researched.

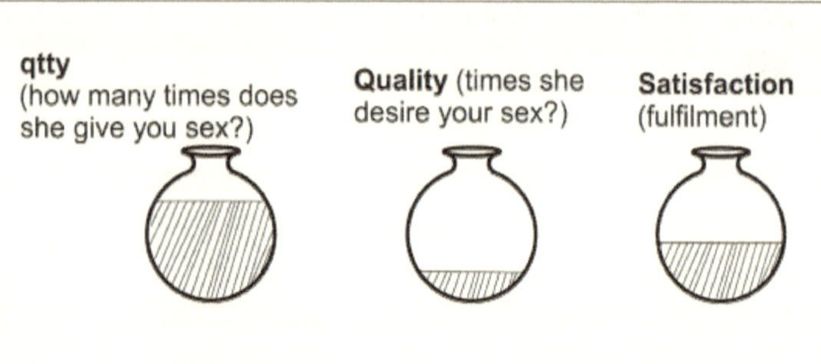

Question is, what happens after the period where the things the man does as duty are no longer needed? When you have built them a proper house? When the children grow and fly out of the country and no longer depend on you? When their mother can go abroad for months and they will take care of her? Isn't this the perpetual story of men abandoned after retirement? Isn't it the man retiring from work and the wife retiring from bedroom work as well? So after a few years of trying to keep up with his many times a week appetite, what my high school chemistry teacher used to call "*lokri kocha*", turn that side, she feels pressured to retire from 'bedroom work'. You retire from your formal work, she retires from working for you. That's my suspicion from the many stories of abandoned old men. They were apart yet together.

So let us say you as the man realize this is not right. It doesn't serve you, it doesn't serve her and it generally doesn't build oneness in the home. It does not accommodate her individuality, her need for pleasure. So you artificially demand less. Try the experiment. Absence creates fondness. Too much of something is poisonous. All of a sudden she blossoms, say she only needs once a week, a nice one once a week. It may even make her want a little more. It builds the relationship and all of a sudden you are her considerate knight in shining armor. You gain more satisfaction from knowing you have got what she needs. But the need for more sex, of good quality won't disappear for this kind of man. There is still a gap! Some even say the reduced sex shortens your life! Once again, this is not a hypothesis about all men. Just a few.

This is what our forefathers saw. Balance. The other woman brings balance. Your great grandmother who was paid for twenty cows brought your great grandfather a next wife to help her keep the man. I can hear some triggered woman shout "she was not educated". Yes, you are right, she did not do a degree like you but she had a PhD in how to be a wife. There's a high likelihood that you cannot halfway compete with the woman she was yet she brought your ancestor a co-wife. She was ten times wife material yet she brought a co-wife. That's why polygamy in Africa worked! Then the white man came with his roman cultured Christianity and poisoned our society. Sowed seeds of selfishness that hasn't helped them and has not helped us since and thus poisoned Africa. Otherwise polygamy would have been phased out long ago if it didn't work. So let us say you have a super wife who seeing how the reduced sexual pressure serves her allows you to bring in another. In short you have a mature, selfless wife who realizes the struggle you are going through to allow her to be herself. As one politician lady in Kenya from Samburu put it, monogamy is selfishness. So she allows you and agrees to share. And you find one who doesn't have the selfishness of monogamy mentality.

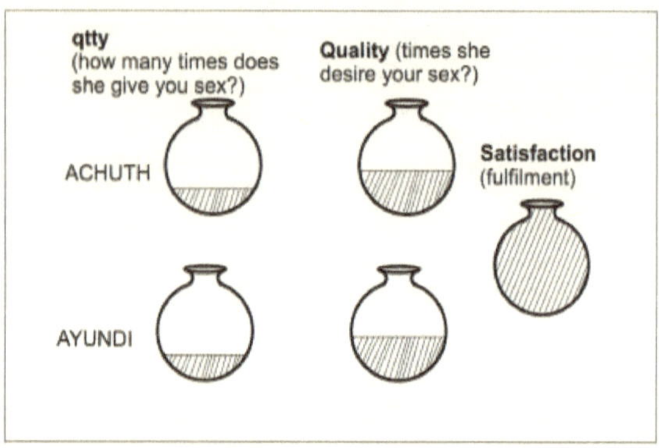

And that is what I believe my forefathers saw. Christianity was supposed to improve it not abolish it! Every person would be doing the much they can. Christianity would make it better.

The phrase "forsaking all others" peddles huge misconceptions. On one side, it's a promise to the man that the lady is sexually equal to him and she will stay so forever. That sexually she is as big an opportunity as two or three of four or five ladies or "a few". The other misconception to the woman is that a man's high sexual desire is an artificial construct that can naturally be frozen without consequences. That he really doesn't need sex. That it is just a mere evil mischievous want. Another misconception is that a pastor's blessing miraculously blunts a man's desire, changes his biology in a way that Muslim marriage and traditional marriage doesn't. In short, Christian men exhibit libido equal to that of women. Polygamy is for the man who wants more feminine attention from wives who want less masculine pressure. It's *kidogo kidogo hujaza kibaba*. Little little satisfies big. And the pressure is real. You hear women discussing a failed marriage they know of and they are saying, "she cooked, she gave birth, she took care, she...." the things I would lump together as nurture. Nurture is great but it can never replace nature. The nature of a man to value sex. And men will never confess that *hashibi*. A man who needs sex marries. It's the biggest thing making men marry. Men who don't need sex should join Apostle Paul. Christianity has groomed men to never admit to being unsatisfied. If you are not satisfied pastors say you lack self-control.

So I believe that I speak for some men out there, selfish enough to admit that the answer to the commonly asked question, "*nyinyi wanaume mnataka nini?*" is simple, enough satisfying sex from one wife if possible, if not then sharing is caring. Aside from the nurture. It gave our grandfathers long life and it will benefit your man. So say the doctors. Maybe this is why 80 year old polygamists are burying hardworking ambitious 50 year old monogamist sons from lifestyle diseases while the errant womanizing son lives longer. The doctors say men sleep better after sex. And quality sleep helps men live longer. If all other things are done but the man is unsatisfied at home he will be walking around a tempted man even before any temptress crosses his path. It is often the case that the man is labeled the evil party yet many are afraid to speak of less satisfaction at home. Nobody holds women accountable for not satisfying the man's sexual needs and I think it is because it is expected that most of them won't. Monogamy as a law was for pastors and deacons and bishops. I am not sure that if you have that calling you must be special enough and that God will give you one special just like you who will quench all your passion. In modern society all sexual related conflicts are first judged as the result of male need misconstrued as greed.

Telling men to be satisfied borders delusion. If someone is hungry he has bought *ugali*. you serve him the *ugali*. Then you tell him he can only pinch it once in a day and that in the mean time he be satisfied by faith. Will be wrong if I accuse you of torture? This i actually see as mental castration.

If you have gotten to the point where his constant banging is too much for your bones then consider sharing him with someone. Sharing is caring. If he went and got you an assistant or two, please, instead of killing yourself with bitterness forgive him and them and thank them for helping you keep that provider alive. Do you know that in the days of your great grandmothers those wise ladies would detect it's time to get the man another girl and they would get one? Nobody forced them and it wasn't the result of lack of western education or Christianity. Your great step-grandmother brought her husband a co-wife who became your great grandmother. That is what a real original traditional woman is. Some tribes still teach and practice that wisdom. Those were based women. Such a culture should not be castigated. Lucky are you, oh man if you have such a wife. She wasn't merely born, she was delicately lowered from heaven! The church has taught our women feminism and its selfishness which is not African. At the same time it has succeeded in teaching a masculinity that serves this feminism. A masculinity that is subdued, begging, grovelling and waiting for sexual favours from the spouse, the famous description of a lion eating grass, no roar, manicured claws with cutex, just looks like a lion, aptly fits that masculinity. Then as the lion chews grass it sees lions on the other hills, thrilled by their roars as they eat meat asks the lioness and pastor lion who are his only company what that is and if he is like them and the lion is told that is hell's property.

The roles of a man are to provide, to protect and to procreate. He has forsaken providing for any other woman to exclusively provide for you. Forsaken protecting other women to protect you. All that with the promise that he will get as much as he needs to keep off the temptation for others. So if you want him to get less from you then God accepted that he can get another less from another person. And your less, dear lady, plus her less plus the other less and your Akuku danger is happy. That's the win win philosophy that I see. Polygamy is born from sexual need, not sexual greed.

A normal man thinks of sex a lot. Even in war. Even when broke. Even without a wife. Some weird ones even when grieving. I think there are very few things like hunger that kills off that urge in men. And not having a woman to think of definitely renders a man impotent. If a woman cannot contain her man's urge it is not wrong to allow him to get another. Otherwise let's ask ourselves. What would be preferable, friendly desirable fulfillment or regular platonic marital contractual work in the bedroom that is sometimes coerced, sometimes even violent which strains the relationship, or cheating where a man hooks up with anyone and anything in secret, or even prostitutes? If just looking at your wife's face would make your erection go down, the world would have been a very peaceful place. If looking at a beautiful face was satisfaction then marriage would be eternal bliss. Our forefathers saw this and were real to the situation. No need to force people in the name of faith which they don't have. No need to force men to pretend they are mini angels. And as am going to demonstrate, God took care of it in the bible.

DOES GOD CHANGE?

So. What does the bible say?

Many state that if God was to allow polygyny then he would have made two or more Eves. Well, the proposers of this theory forget that Eve was perfect. She was not created with the biological issues we now see. So it is true that monogamy is the standard in Eden. Well, guess what, they fell from perfection when they sinned. And so did death and decay enter earth. So if women are as perfect as Eve and the men as perfect as Adam, then they can last 900 years or even forever together banging each other. If you are talking of biology beyond Eden and past the flood, just be real. The key ingredient of masculinity is realism. It is the foundation of logic. Even in facing God he says "come let us reason". By this not to mean throw reality out of the window but let us look at it together. If a is community commanded by people who casually dismiss reality then the community degenerates into delusion as is evident in the western civilization.

The first mention of polygamy is Genesis 4:19. Cain's grandson Lamech married Adah and Zillah. I can guess what you are about to say, "You see, it came from Cain! Evil!" It is noteworthy that God doesn't call it evil or good. Is it because God is being nice and doesn't want to disturb good people? Are you referring to the same God who had just punished Cain? Was God afraid of correcting this new "vice"? Was God looking aside, afraid, as one man's greed and selfishness invented something so diabolical and would distort humanity for all its existence? The bible says in Acts 10:34. God is not a respecter of persons. If God was abetting evil then that would make him a respecter of man. It would make him God shaped by man. A man-made God. A mere idol. Kindly note that these people were still few in number. It would be illogical to think that He who shortly after destroyed the world with flooding was unable to tell mankind that he didn't want polygamy. At all times we must remember that God is not some celebrity on social media thirsty for likes and smileys. He said that if we refuse to praise him the stones will sing his praises. He has the power to press the delete button doing away with imperfection and copy pasting perfection instantly. Thus it is okay to conclude that this was done with God's approval. Lamech's crime was to murder and not to marry two wives. How could a monogamist Adam give birth to a polygamist? Same way Adam and Eve are the source of all Chinese, Africans, Caucasians, Mumbuti and all.

Then we get to the case of Jacob and Esau. Both sons of Isaac were polygamists. Esau's wives made his parents sad (genesis 26:34-35). This was a case of two wrong choices. Rebekah's analysis in genesis 27:48 points to this fact. She further states that should Jacob get even one of such it will be a disaster. *Rivkah said to Yitz'chak, "I'm sick to death of Hitti women! If Ya'akov marries one of the Hitti women, like those who live here, my life won't be worth living."* (CJB). Even one of those women was living poison. Esau had two. Up until when Jacob was being sent away Esau didn't realize his wives were toxic. So he added a third. He did the godly thing. He didn't divorce. Jacob is told to get a wife he ends up with four. Was it by mistake? Or was it by God's design? Was God busy distracted while his promise carriers were busy messing up?

Anyone thinking that God was just allowing stuff to happen without an opinion is accusing God of simping. If he follows the whims of men and is afraid if tripping men then he truly is made God by man. And God is no simp. If it is evil he says it's evil. He fears nobody. He who warned Cain and flooded the earth is not a respecter of persons. He wrestled Jacob. God actually used the polygamy to grow Israel. It was his polygamy.

An important event is recorded in genesis 35:22. Reuben, Jacobs first born has a fling with Jacob's concubine. Here we see the Godly principle set, even if a man has how many wives touching any of them is touching his wives. It is adultery. There is no extra wife.

Many associate the mention of polygamy with evil and say that polygamy is evil because some polygamists in the bible did evil. I dispute this, it is wrong to believe so because if it is murder then where is Cain's other wives? The guy was a monogamist. Jacob was a schemer, yes. That was him, he did that before he married any wife. The interpretation that polygamy is innately evil is just looking at the bible using Roman spectacles. What of Ahab? Wasn't he a monogamist? And jeroboam? And Manasseh? How many evil monogamists are there in the bible?

And before I forget, how many wives did Adam have? Just one? He damned humanity because of his one wife? Let me be cheeky and suggest that if he had two or three wives we would still be in Eden running around stark naked and Eve's grave would have been in a corner to remind us never to go near that damned fruit. If Adam believed God could give him another wife and he refused to eat with Eve they would have been the first discordant couple of the world. One infected with sin another not infected. Should we then conclude that monogamy makes men devils? It destroyed Adam and the whole humanity!

And this misconception about polygamy has caused many sorrows. Wives thrown out in the name of salvation, children left fatherless in the name of Jesus. Evil that should never be associated with God. This book is the African spectacles looking at the matter.

Then came the legislation on polygamy. But before I delve into it, if you stole my goat and as you were cutting it up next to my fence I found you but instead of calling the police I told you "just bring two legs and one side of the ribs." what would you conclude? That you are guilty or forgiven and accepted?

Let me use a scene from the movie Life. The setting is in the 40s. Someone has impregnated the white prison superintendent's daughter. All the prisoners are black. The furious superintendent lines them up in a parade holding the baby against each inmate in a bid to nab the baby daddy. Midway his daughter causes a commotion after which one by one each inmate declares the child is his culminating in the hilarious words, "I da pappy", from Jangle Leg (played by Bernie Mac). They all owned that child. The child's status changed from an illegitimate child to a child owned that very moment.

You may claim, oh, many tribes had this practices before this and oh, God.... Well, I have news for you. When God accepts something he is owning it. He is saying "I da pappy". What he accepts he does so because he owns it from the beginning. It wasn't some random idea, it wasn't a fluke, God, Jesus, da pappy. It was his idea, his design and as He legislated it he was stipulating how he designed it to be. God cannot plagiarize man and if he did he is a man-made God. This God can plant a baby in a womb without the process of sex therefore planting a thought in someone's mind is no big deal.

Leviticus 18:18. You shall not marry a woman as a rival to her sister. Also exodus 21:10 when one adds a wife the provision, protection, privileges of the first wife shouldn't be reduced. In short, God allows polygamy but when entering polygamy one was not allowed to marry sisters. Since God cannot be made wise by men I can only conclude that God accepted polygamy because he made it. Any practice of polygamy prior to that mentioned in the Torah is there because God created it. In short by legislating polygamy God was not merely accepting polygamy but more important owning it as his idea and as I shall show he even required it in some cases.

Put in other words polygamy is an equal standard alongside monogamy and celibacy before God. Many say, "oooh, but that is old testament". Really? Isn't this the same God who says he does not change? And where is that recorded? Isn't it the old testament? There's this notion of Old Testament versus New Testament. And it subtly pushes across the notion that God changed somewhere. That in the Old Testament he was simping with a patriarchal society, dynastic leaning, concerned with government, business and wars. That his command then was multiply and subdue the earth. Then he went for holiday , thought things over, came back in the new testament commonly depicted by many as a woke activist, feminist, communist God and one whose new command is if you are not proselytizing the world you are not his and he would we all were like Paul.

God did not go on holiday between the testaments and then came back changed. He added salvation to what was. He fulfilled the promise of replacing salvation through animal sacrifice with the blood of Christ. He fulfilled salvation beyond Jewish lineage. He fulfilled direct relationship without human intermediaries. He fulfilled circumcision of the heart. He freed worship of Adonai from being about Jerusalem. He did not change. He is the same. Delete the New Testament Old Testament dichotomy from your mind.

Jesus is not God version 2.0 but the same Jesus, God, who gave Moses the law. Jesus gave Moses what Moses got on Mt. Sinai. As he says, *before Abraham was I AM*. This is the African spectacles. Stop telling me of old and New Testament, as if there's old and new God. I have one bible flowing from Genesis to revelation. Someone should try it one day. Print The African Bible that lacks that separation. In fact once I realized this I went ahead and tore out that page written New Testament and the one written Old Testament from my favorite copy of the bible. I keep those pages hung somewhere to remind me that God doesn't change. What is the separation really for? What he cared for in Genesis, doesn't he care for in revelation? What he called sin in exodus, doesn't He still call sin in Corinthians? What he allowed in Leviticus doesn't he still allow in Matthew?

Actually historically some claim that the first to use a canon with a form of the New Testament was Marcion, later counted a heretic. He dismissed the Old Testament in totality. And indeed he held that Jesus was different and opposed to the Old Testament "Creator God". How can something founded in such a heretic view have been inspired by God? Didn't Jesus himself tell us a house divided against itself cannot stand? Do not tell me that I will understand how the dichotomy came by faith. Any time someone says "understand by faith" I ask myself where did Jesus tell someone to understand something by faith? Jesus is truth. Truth never needs faith to understand. Believing needs faith, understanding needs reasoning. Use faith where believing is needed. I have come to realize it is prudent to believe after understanding. Understanding is the donkey that carries belief. Putting faith before understanding is like faith carrying on its head the donkey it should be riding. Where reasoning is needed do not bring faith bring the brains God gave you. Kindly note that the greatest defence that every "woke" person uses to dismiss common sense usually starts with, "you don't understand". Delusion starts when you use faith where you need logic.

Indeed by our words we speak of one God but by what we believe about him we express an old testament, more African accepting, more partriachal, Jewish friendly God and a new testament Roman cultured Christian God. We tell everyone we worship one God, yet we express an obsolete Old Testament God and a current New Testament God. It is like those men who officially have one wife but his polygamous status is an open secret. Marcion's canon consisted of a shorter version of the gospel of Luke and Paul's epistles. Sounds familiar?

When the all Jewish Jerusalem council met they in essence unburdened Christians from converting to Judaism to please Jesus. However, it seemed that the councils under the reign of Constantine were hellbent on redefining Roman culture as the culture of Christianity.

The basis on which polygamy is stigmatized in the church is Marcionism to the core. Seriously, how can this be the proposer of new-testament-Vs-old-testament type of thinking!?

To further stress this point let us talk more of how God demonstrates that his standards are perfect. Psalm 19:7 - 9

7The law of the LORD is perfect,
Refreshing the soul.
The statutes of the LORD are trustworthy,
Making wise the simple.

8 The precepts of the LORD are right,
Giving joy to the heart.
The commands of the LORD are radiant,
Giving light to the eyes.

9 The fear of the LORD is pure,
Enduring forever.
The decrees of the LORD are firm,
And all of them are righteous.

God says his laws are perfect, his statutes are right, they are trustworthy. And I have come to admit that in the whole of existence God does not bend to culture. He is too great for that. It is we with our wicked woke mentality who must accept that he in his sovereignty and wisdom, accepted something that we find obnoxious. Even Paul said *All Scripture is God-breathed and is valuable for teaching the truth, convicting of sin, correcting faults and training in right living; thus anyone who belongs to God may be fully equipped for every good work.* 2 Timothy 3: 16, 17(CJB). Kindly note that Paul was summarizing psalm 19: 7-9. And also note that the scripture he was referring to was what we dismissively call the Old Testament and the life of Christ. All those miracle-performing, demon chasing Christians in the book of Acts had one canon, a Jesus approved cannon, starting with genesis ending in Malachi, that they did not call old. The Jewish sacrifice and people were of the old circumcision agreement, covenant, but that scripture was not all circumcision and sacrifice. Other than the heretic Marcion, I have yet to hear any scholar speak of one who was given the inspiration for that dichotomy. I was only told to accept it because I was never allowed to question it.

Another biblical legislation found in the bible is Deuteronomy 17:17

He must not take many wives, or his heart will be led astray. He must not accumulate large amounts of silver and gold.

The 'he' referred to here is the king. If God hates polygamy then here he missed a big chance to stop it. There was no king yet and there would not be for over a century later. He was creating the culture of royalties. What would you understand by the words 'not ... many'? If you asked me how many people I found in a room and I told you they were not many, would you conclude I mean that I found only one person? If you were serving *mahamri* at the self-service counter and I told you don't take many, would you understand you should only take one or would you understand, a few, don't be greedy?

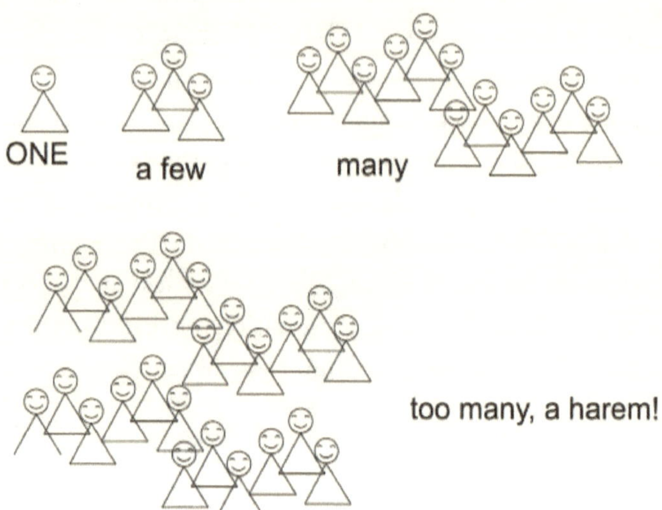

Just to demonstrate how God stays the same, take the example of slavery. Many purport that in the book of Exodus God was bending to culture, that it wasn't time to abolish slavery. And now that man is modern God is like "hey, I didn't like it either, it was the fashion back then." Are you sure? The Israelites had just been miraculously emancipated from painful racially motivated slavery. This was the most perfect time to show the world that God does not accept slavery. They had fresh wounds on their bodies from slavery. A whole generation of children had been killed. They were beaten, shaken, pressed but not destroyed. The whole community was a community of ex slaves from the greatest to the least. Apart from Moses. Allow me to use the emancipation declaration for a parallel. Imagine that God, after devastating America, instructs the ex-slaves to cross the Atlantic back to Liberia. Then as part of the brand new constitution penned by God himself, God gives them laws on how to conduct slavery. Imagine their Moses is Martin Luther King jr., reading regulations about slavery to a crowd of Malcolm Xs, Jomo Kenyattas, Oginga Odingas, Kwame Nkrumahs, Julius Nyereres, Mandelas, Samora Machels and you my black or African brother. Imagine you are part of the emancipated crowd below!

Just imagine! This was totally counter to the prevailing situation! This is exactly what happened. Psalm 19 wasn't written in the 1800s. He says his decrees are firm. You know what "firm" means? That he doesn't change his standards. Leviticus is full of laws on slavery, God allowed slavery. Did he change? No. Turn to the New Testament and you find the book of Philemon. The book of Philemon is actually about one born again Christian owning another born again Christian as a slave and Paul reconciling the two! And you know what? God owns it. Psalm 116:16 *Oh, Adonai ! I am your slave; I am your*

slave, the son of your slave-girl; you have removed my fetters. The best of us are God's slaves. God was not ignoring it for the sake of cultural appropriateness. For decades I was unable to wrap my mind around this story and the illogical explanations I was getting about God being culturally correct. Till I finally accepted that whatever God accepts, he has accepted in his unquestionable sovereign wisdom and he didn't consult us or our foolish cultures. If I say he bent to culture then he is weak. How can the one who destroyed Sodom before the book of Romans was written, the one who released the flood, how can he be scared to stop slavery? He does not change! Do you want to tell me God shifts standards according to human culture? Or he only shifted for Arabs and Europeans? Does he then shift for the Indians? Does he shift for.... LGBTQ? Why didn't he shift then to accommodate Africans if he has been shifting through history? Or he stopped shifting and settled when he interacted with the extremely civilized Europe whose culture amazed Him? There is an undeniable racial component to the theory of God looking aside to accommodate some cultures and not accommodate other cultures. Actually monogamy as a rule was Christianity being bent to fit Roman culture.

The day God changes his standards he stops being God. He says he is perfect. The alpha and omega. What does perfect God have to perfect in? If you can prove God changes standards then you will have proven He is not God. Christian justification for laws against slavery is not that God doesn't permit slavery but that it became inhuman. Any Christian trying to say God bends to culture is just humansplaining God. God is not like a mighty ruler who has to dish out favors so as to remain on the throne, he is not a man, stop it. One Alka

Mbumba put it so well in his song "Fanda nayo". No one voted to make God who he is, he isn't God because people chose him. He doesn't need to give bribes nor dish out political favors. He doesn't need the approval of men.

Another example is when Jesus speaks about divorce. In the Old Testament Jesus permitted divorce through the laws given to Moses. In the New Testament he explains that he hates it, but this is where he shows again he is God. In that he doesn't withdraw his permission. In short he doesn't change even over what he hates. What he permits is permitted forever. What he loves he loves forever. And he himself has bound himself and said *God is not man, that he should lie, or a son of man, that he should change his mind* (Numbers 23:19 ESV). He says nobody has added him wisdom. Man does not come up with ideas that enlighten God and add God experience. It is I and you who should stop humansplaining God and see him in his majesty and sovereignty enthroned above us and not shaped and bent by our fashions and trends.

And by the way, Jesus said after divorce one should marry again. So how do you explain marriage after divorce that you allow? How? Isn't it obvious that the polygamy provision is a better solution to this problem of adultery that divorce brings? I have never heard a solid reasoning behind this. Indeed when monogamy is made the law it drags along divorce together with so many vices just the way a shadow follows each one of us. Divorce is part of the shadow of what we call Christian marriage. And the numbers don't lie.

And what did God say of idols? They cannot talk! So God can talk for himself? Oh yes. He himself says so using his own mouth. People who came up with the notion that God is insinuating polygamy is evil forget that that is the crime of reducing God to an idol who must be spoken for. What he forbade yesterday he forbids today. What he allowed yesterday, he allows today. He is the creator of perfect celibacy, the creator of perfect monogamy and the creator of perfect polygamy. Yes, that exists.

Many depict the verses that I have mentioned as if God was hinting that he is uncomfortable with polygamy but was not saying so directly. As far as am concerned this is a refusal to accept what God accepts. God has never shied from telling man he hates something. These notions reduce the eminence and majesty of God to the level of weak men married to feminists who do not speak up and do not take action in the house. As if God is under happy human happy God law. He allowed divorce but said categorically that he hates divorce. He clearly gave the disclaimer. If he was uncomfortable with talking of polygamy then at that point he missed a great chance to. But what if he isn't uncomfortable with it like certain cultures? If you accept that he is okay with polygamy then it makes perfect sense that he not talk about it. If he has nothing to add about polygamy then please don't add for him. He is not an idol. And isn't it curious that the divorce God hates is more accepted by the church than the polygamy he has no issues with? Africa, wake up, before the continent, still in poverty, is as divorced as the west. Anyone who makes monogamy a rule is preaching divorce. As a standard is okay but as a rule and a law it makes the saying 'marriage is the greatest cause of divorce' very accurate.

Other laws in the bible show that God actually required it of men. First one I see is Deuteronomy 25 about wife inheritance. If the man with the right to redeem refuses God's instruction was that she would take the case to the elders. If he still refuses after they talk to him; *9 his brother's widow shall go up to him in the presence of the elders, take off one of his sandals, spit in his face and say, "This is what is done to the man who will not build up his brother's family line." 10 That man's line shall be known in Israel as The Family of the Unsandaled.* That's a pretty harsh treatment. And even having married already was not accepted as an excuse. Your dead brother's wife was required to spit on your face under instruction from God! Godly spitting of spite. God despised the one who had an excuse to refuse. And your descendants would be shamed for it forever! This was not God accepting an existing culture in Israel but God creating the culture. He was not rubber stamping what the Israelites were doing but starting what they were to do. Those instructions in the books of Moses are not God accepting culture but God creating culture. He created that culture. He did not bend to it. Anyone claiming God bent to culture is in effect insulting God's grace.

Also as William Luck noted about Exodus 22:16 that if a man seduces a woman not betrothed he must marry her subject only to the girl's father's disapproval. In short even being married is not an excuse. Same law given concerning defiling a virgin. I find this such a high standard but if we accepted that this was an instruction from God then there would be less or no single parented children in Christian dominated and Christian influenced societies. The empirical evidence is that wherever Christianity goes, so does single motherhood. This requirement placed responsibility on the man for starting the relationship. The result was forcibly marry or pay bride price. It also placed responsibility on the holder of keys to unlock sex, the woman. The result for her was forced to be a wife or shamefully be paid for bride price. Indeed God had a solution. You eat her precious reserved cookies whether or not you impregnate her you marry her unless the father says no. It also points out the role of the father. Someone show me where did Jesus cancel this instruction? In short a disgraced father is owed not just child support but bride price.

Another thing that I note, whatever God has declared is married no man dare divorce. Therefore if God declares that by sleeping with a marriageable woman she is your wife save for if her dad says no, then the church monogamy law creates divorces all over called baby mamas. God hates divorce. God calls it violence. The church is thus complicit in multiplying baby mama which is indeed divorce. How can Jesus be the excuse people are using to technically divorce after cheating girls? In this matter doesn't many of our African traditions align with the bible? Would our ancestors have allowed someone to impregnate their daughter with no consequence? I know mine didn't because I come from a clan whose story starts with a refugee who impregnated his host's daughter. He was forced to marry her.

The church killed moral responsibility by replacing the God given father's permanent prominent position in the marriage and sexuality complex of daughters with a stranger, the pastor, who can be replaced and has no God given authority as concerns a woman's vows. Sometimes the pastor is even another woman. It is clear that the authority is with the father not the pastor, Numbers 30:3-5 *"When a young woman still living in her father's household makes a vow to the Lord or obligates herself by a pledge and her father hears about her vow or pledge but says nothing to her, then all her vows and every pledge by which she obligated herself will stand. But if her father forbids her when he hears about it, none of her vows or the pledges by which she obligated herself will stand; the Lord will release her because her father has forbidden her-*(NIV).

There's a big reason why men fear pastors. They steal the honour of both fathers and husbands. According to God marriage starts when the father says yes not when the pastor says kiss the bride. If he says no then it is no even before God. Even if you elope. Pastors are transient. Fathers are irreplaceable. I hear father is the first boyfriend a girl has. Not pastor. That thing of spiritual father and spiritual mother is a modern version of Mark 7:11-13 *But you say that if anyone declares that what might have been used to help their father or mother is Corban (that is, devoted to God)— And he continued, "You have a fine way of setting aside the commands of God in order to observe your own traditions! For Moses said, 'Honor your father and mother,' and, 'Anyone who curses their father or mother is to be put to death.' then you no longer let them do anything for their father or mother. Thus you nullify the word of God by your tradition that you have handed down. And you do many things like that."*NIV. I have heard preachers say that for a wedding to proceed all they need is the bride, the groom, the certificate, a witness and an officiating pastor. Please note that God recognises the father as solemniser of marriage not the pastor. That one is Roman tradition passed down generation to generation. By declaring the honor of a father corban we water down chastity. Your pastor is not your father. Never will be, unless they raised you and guided you through every stage. If they played the father role. Unless they disciplined you, dear girl, for talking to a boy in the maize fields and they can demand bride price.

Jesus did not speak what many call the old covenant from the right side of his mouth and the new from the left. He himself said he didn't come to erase what he had said in ages past but to fulfill it. What is the difference between calling it "old covenant" and calling it "obsolete covenant"? If I say, "My old shirt, my old TV, my old self, my old table", and then I say, "my new shirt, my new TV, my new self"; am I not insinuating that there's something obsolete and something else currently useful? Isn't it saying the old is like those cars kept somewhere gathering dust while we occasionally harvest spare parts of verses for tithing and promises of success? Isn't it implying that there is something that has sentimental value but no authority? Reminds me of one day I was at Owino market in Kampala. That day the Kabaka was walking in the market. All business stopped as people got out to cheer royalty. then it hit me, as adored as he was the guy is powerless. That's like the old testament. Adored, revered but labeled obsolete. My understanding was the sacrificing for reconciliation was part of all he had said from genesis. What was to be fulfilled, what was temporal was clearly stated. And that he did fulfill by which He opened what was a preserve of one select nation to the whole world.

His dying on the cross does not mean he changed even an iota of the scriptures. I find it delusional to present to the world God who is split in two and then insist that you have one God. I mean, the Old Testament is all about Jehovah and the New Testament about Jesus who isn't mentioned by name in the Old Testament. The only way Jesus is Jehovah is if there is no that Roman minded bible division. And when I really question you tell me to have faith. Faith cannot be a substitute for illogical thinking. Faith does not negate logic. And don't talk of circumcision, it was a practice and he definitely said not a must. He neither stopped it nor required it of the rest of the world. He fulfilled the covenant from a circumcision covenant to the cross being my circumcision. He fulfilled the covenant from being a Jerusalem temple covenant to being a New Jerusalem covenant. He didn't delete the covenant he had with Israel but from his prototype he produced the mass product. He fulfilled it making it a way for the world and not just for Israel. Jesus as God didn't scrap what he gave the Jews, he just did what he did with the 5 fish and 2 loaves, and he used them to feed us all! I realize what was to be fulfilled and what was accepted are two different things.

I wonder, was it a racial thing for the church under Rome to insist on an Old (depicted as partially obsolete) and a New Testament? Imagine you are a Roman. Accepting the things in the Old Testament, admitting that God has a standard for cultures, prototyped in Jewry, would make roman traditions subservient to Jewish culture. In fact imagine telling your proud Romans who have Jewish slaves that now your priests are going to be priests of Yahweh God of Abraham, Isaac and Jacob. Didn't they just defeat that God horribly and selling off those descendants of Avraham, Y'itzak and Y'akov that they didn't kill? There is no way a conqueror can accept the culture of their conquered slaves to be the filter of what is acceptable. Accepting what many call the Old Testament at par with what they called the new would elevate the status of these conquered Jews. It would demand much cultural humbling.

Solution, declare part of the bible as semi obsolete. Behave like a worldly second wife or third wife, which they actually were. Tell the world you are the current and only love. The first wife, Jewry, many Christians believe, is divorced and now Christianity, the new wife, runs the house. Just the same way the new young brides would behave. Despising the other wife she found there. She looks at her and says to herself "I have been brought in because this one is hard headed". Isn't that the same attitude Christians have held to Jews for ages? Isn't that the prevailing replacement theory? I believe it's time I have one bible with 66 books all currently in use. I told you God is a polygamist. Israel and Judah are his *mikai* and *nyachira*, (the first and second wives among the Luo). Roman Christianity the third, protestants the fourth, charismatics somewhere there. All have unique identities but all united in Christ, God, as his one bride.

At the same time the first wife, Jewry, denounces the others as lost and following false doctrine. If you claim that there is only one church identity, I see many. Facts are facts. If I can count them then that is statistically called many. It is their unity that makes them one bride, one universal church, one family, even the groom prayed that they will be united, not a bunch of squabbling wives. And that bride is grafted onto the old vine of Jewry. The bible talks of "the house of David". One house. Singular in spite of his many wives. Though many they are united in one Christ. Just as Jesus said, be one as I and the Father are one. Someone intended that we overlook the fact that roman embrace of Christianity as the state religion was not out of conviction but out of mere political convenience. So how much do you trust the works of politicians? How much do you trust the compromises made so as to politically accommodate roman superior master position within the Christian circles? The same passed down as to be understood without question by faith? Rome in my view was intent in introducing Christ as a roman deity and not as the creator the Jews worship. I am not advocating for Jewish legalism but whatever God accepts in the template he gave jews that's in my culture should not be demonized simply because it isn't European compliant.

Denying that that culture was made and defined by God, Adonai, is denying God exists. The view that God was plagiarizing the thoughts of man and claiming them to be his own wisdom is blasphemously claiming men made God.

Another law that touches on this is you shall not commit adultery. Many have theorized that polygamy is adultery. Well if polygamy is adultery then war is murder. And spies must never disguise themselves or lie. You cannot commit adultery with your wife. If her father or family, those mandated to receive bride price, accept you as her husband whether she is your first or your second or third she is your wife. Some say that the woman at the well whom Jesus spoke to was sinning by being a second wife. I dare to say that Jesus said the man had not married her. Meaning she had given up on marriage and was now on come we stay and see if it will work. So does adultery still apply to polygamy? Yes! If she has not been married to the man then she is not a wife. Sleeping with one you cannot marry, have not married and have no intention of marrying is adultery. No one can commit adultery with his wife. Even if it's the fourth wife.

Secondly. Sleeping with a woman married to another man is adultery. Just ask David. That was what brought evil to his previously peaceful home. Note that till then he had a perfectly peaceful home. God had given him a home where nobody wanted to kill the other. They were okay. Adultery destroys both monogamy and polygamies.

So, do we find examples in the new testament keeping with consistency that what God allows he is too wise to wisen up somewhere along the way and change concerning polygamy? Oh yes. 1 Timothy 3:2a. [2] *A bishop then must be blameless, the husband of one wife*, Many have used this verse to explain that everyone should uphold the standard of the bishop thus this is a clear law stating monogamy. I beg to differ. If I tell you, go to the fruit basket and among the fruits only pick the oranges to make juice, what would you understand? That the basket only has oranges? No. it means that there are other fruits, bananas, pineapples, mangoes, coconuts (am still not sure that's a fruit) in the basket. But because i want orange juice get oranges. So by saying only those with one wife are permitted in church leadership it means there are polygamists in that pew as well and not specified how they got into it.

You may argue that the word polygamy isn't used. We are often times guilty of looking at historical times using our woke modern standards. Thus this verse being read using modern teachings sounds like a monogamy instruction yet go back in time to when it was written and you find very African like Jews. As soon as Timothy read Paul's letter he knew that Ochola,

Otieno and Odhoch with their many wives could not be bishops.

Well, at the same time if that argument insists that one must marry one wife, it then also excludes celibacy which isn't mentioned there as well. That would clash with the rest of the verses. That argument also fails horribly on another front, are we supposed to be images of bishops or Jesus? So why do you want members to be images of bishops? I can hear someone shout "well, Paul said follow me as I follow Christ", true. That is Paul, not any bishop. And Paul wasn't married so is that bishop celibate? Does the bishop have books in the bible so that we use his following of Christ as a standard? If we followed every bishop won't there be confusion? So as long as any bishop convinces me he is following Christ i follow that bishop? The "me" was Paul and still is Paul. Never believe that because you went to theology school the bible was given to us through you the way it was given to Paul. That was the mistake that kept the bible in Latin till William Tyndale came along. And those preachers burnt him at the stake for the crime of robbing them of the position of self-appointed intermediaries. Why do we have such a huge crowd sewing the veil back? Jesus tears it apart, others quickly pick threads and needles.

Then we move on to some very positive examples from polygamy. The first is Samuel. One may argue that there was rivalry in the family. Well, I have come to learn that women don't have to be married to one man for them to be rivals and to quarrel. Were Euodia and Syntyche married to the same man? Maybe, we aren't told. If you are looking at it with Roman eyes it's impossible. But if you look at it with African eyes, maybe. Safe to assume they weren't. They don't even have to be married at all. They will find points to be rivals. God comes to bring peace where chaos reigns. However God chooses this polygamy family, to raise one of the greatest prophets. We will revisit this story when we discuss the perfect polygamy. Because, yes, in Jesus it exists otherwise Jesus would be irrelevant to polygamy families.

For God so loved the world. That includes polygnies. There are some aspects that am sure you never hear about Elkanah's family. Majorly because preaching to polygamy families has been a taboo. A stumbling block introduced by westernization of this beautiful gospel. The bible is capable of integrating any culture. It is a refiner of cultures. It is not western culture.

Now let me introduce an observation that really crimson pilled me. Turn to Jeremiah 3.

6 During the reign of King Josiah, the LORD said to me, "Have you seen what faithless Israel has done? She has gone up on every high hill and under every spreading tree and has committed adultery there. 7 I thought that after she had done all this she would return to me but she did not, and her unfaithful sister Judah saw it. 8 I gave faithless Israel her certificate of divorce and sent her away because of all her adulteries. Yet I saw that her unfaithful sister Judah had no fear; she also went out and committed adultery. 9 Because Israel's immorality mattered so little to her, she defiled the land and committed adultery with stone and wood. 10 In spite of all this, her unfaithful sister Judah did not return to me with all her heart, but only in pretense," declares the LORD.

Here God, Jesus, creates an image where he is married to two ladies. Israel and Judah. As a young man this example stirred my thoughts. God, the polygamist? Impossible! But there it is so whoever thinks God hates polygamy, please erase those words from His Word if you can. That image is what is called polygamy. That's how he divorced one then the other. God is telling us that His bride is one but the one is made up of many. He has a relationship with us as individuals and with the church as one. The church is a bride consisting of many identities but so unified as to be called one bride. He said be one as I and The father are one. Meaning, He, Jesus, admitted that there will be many diverse identities but they must identify as one. There are Presbyterians, catholic, Anglicans, Lutherans, Baptists, others with names that sound like a sentence, all accessing Christ directly. It is their oneness that qualifies them to be one bride. So where do men get the polygamous capability? From the person who wrote Jeremiah 3:6-10. And just like God their father some are endowed with ability to love more than one. And some are endowed with ability to be Christ loving co-wives who love each other. It's not an anomaly or a miracle.

After analyzing all these I have concluded that the belief in a woke God is foreign to the bible. Personally, to me, he who can prove that Jesus hates polygamy and even slavery will have proven to me that Jesus is not Jehovah. Or else one will have to prove that as God, Jesus, was giving Moses the law, that He later called perfect, that this was not part of the perfect or it wasn't Yahweh's words. There are no grey areas in this. It's either Jesus is I AM, Jehovah, or he is not.

UNFAIR EQUITY, UNJUST EQUALITY

All men are created equal. So say the Americans and that phrase has since been adopted by all and shaped humanity. Unquestioned. This topic can never be spoken of without speaking of equality.

And I wonder what do we mean when we say all are created equal? Is being born of a woman the basis of equality? If being born is equality then we are also equal to cows, goats and dogs. Aren't they also born? Aren't they conceived in much the same manner? They are even born walking! They are superior to us at birth! How much equality is there beyond being born? Do we all consume the same amount of oxygen? Do we all weigh equal? Do we all look the same? Do we all have equal output? Do we all like the same things? Do we all grow equally? Can we all do the same career? Is pooping what makes us equal? Is eating what makes us equal? Is dying what makes us equal? But even cockroaches eat, poop and die, so are we equal to cockroaches? What is equal in creation?

The term "equal" is a mathematical term. It is used to denote measurable and hence scientific parameters. One kilogram of salt has equal weight to one kilogram of cotton wool. For them to be at equal weight all other parameters scream inequality. It is ironical that equality is the greatest proof of inequality.

I do believe the Americans were reacting to oppression under monarchies. Do remember that this was the period where we had the waning imperial Roman Empire. This was the same time we had King James who believed he ruled as a divine right. The immigrants, I would expect, were thus tired of having nobility by birth. It is thus not surprising that on the new world everyone would want to break those chains of royals with special privilege yet they die like anyone and have toilets like everyone and they don't deposit gold nuggets in them, their toilets too need cleaning.

I also do believe the European and Roman past of the church sneaked in feminism. Before the spread of Christianity the Romans and Greeks and the Vikings had male gods and female gods. Their gods even had wives. The Greek gods even cheated! Which I find hilarious. Thus the concept of non-feminine God really disturbed them. No wonder they elevated Mary to Mary mother of God. The Romans transferred their feminism to Christianity. A result of politically motivated conversion. Having the form but not the power thereof.

So, how do you, in such a situation, introduce basic rights to all? I thus understand that they introduced equal creation as a justification for equal rights. But I do believe rights do not have to be pegged on equal creation. The rights that are universal are universal because it is the creator of all who gave these rights. And in fact rights cannot be equal. They can only be rights. If you have a right to wage it doesn't mean you all earn equal wage. Communism tried equal pay that and failed. The bible provides the best template for rights in my view. Without God people fumble as to what other reason would justify for all to have rights. It is evident that the Roman Republic as well as New Testament Christianity may have influenced that famous equality thought.

Equality is in the business of fronting the argument for fairness. Equity on the other hand fights for justice. Justice and fairness are different. Fairness in my view is founded on "without favoritism, without discrimination."

Justice is about what is deserved. My understanding of fair is giving all the same treatment, assigning all the same value, considering all as being same. Justice on the other hand as I have come to understand has to do with what is deserved, what is earned, what something or someone is worth. In primary school I attended a boarding school. The school was founded on fairness. When it came to meal time each pupil was assigned to a table. Each table had a table leader. The table leader's work was to ensure all plates had the same amount of food. Thus it's obvious the bigger bodied, or hyperactive boys used to get less than they need while those with smaller bodies or were less playful were overfed. Equality gets disturbed by the natural excess while someone else has want. Equality is artificial. We would batter trade items since money was illegal in the school. Things like cuttings in colour of Rambo or Commando(Arnold Schwarzenegger) were priced currencies in exchange for food. the food distribution was fair but it wasn't just. Fairness ignores the reality of inherent inequality of nature.

Equality will tell the animals, "since all animals are equal from today all animals eat grass." After that they discover that the lion, the cheetah, the leopard all cannot digest grass.

So the gazelles tell the lions, "Times have changed, you cannot go on eating meat as if we are in 1800s. These are modern times."

Afterwards it is quietly accepted that the lion's right negates the gazelle rights.

Or even take the example of gold and silver. Equality will insist that 1 kilogram of gold is equal in worth to one kilogram of iron. If i was to apply equality I will insist on exchanging 1 kilogram of iron for 1 kilogram of gold. Would you accept that deal? that because they are equal in weight their value is equal? But let us do a just deal won't your one kilogram of gold buy three tons of my iron? It doesn't mean gold is more useful than iron. It doesn't mean we need more gold. Somehow we need less gold, we have less gold but its just price is equal to tons of the more useful iron. One may say the market value is a human construct. I beg to differ. Kindly note that the creator of the universe ensured the abundance of iron right where we will need it. This is further proof that there is a creator whose wisdom is beyond measure. It is that creator who laid the foundation of inequality where iron is more useful but gold is more precious when he hid the minerals beneath our feet.

Which makes me wonder, when we say we are all created equal do we mean we are all created human? Iron, silver, gold, copper are all metals. Does that make them equal? Do they all weigh the same per a litre of volume? Do they all have the same strength? Are they all magnetic? Do they all react the same way? Do they all do the same jobs? Replacing 'human' with 'equal' is the same lunacy as replacing 'metal' with 'equal'. Even atoms of the same element can be unequal. Chemists call them isotopes. There is hydrogen and heavy hydrogen.

Even consider crops. It is God who decided that a hectare of maize will produce about thrice the tonnage of a hectare of beans. This inequality then shows up in their prices.

To those who argue that it is unfair for a man to have many wives while women can only have one husband I say this another example of God's wisdom. If a man only sleeps with the wife or wives he has married and they are all faithful to him then we can forget about HIV. That is why the law on adultery still applies. I have seen God is just and sovereign. The leopard prays that it will catch a gazelle while the gazelle prays to not be caught. If God were to be fair the leopard would be eating grass. God can do it. But in his sovereignty he elects the unfair inequality of the gazelle being sustenance for the leopard.

Consider the laws and commandments given by God to Moses. At first glance it is a list of 'do's and "don't"s. Viewed from the angle of grace they are the many things for which God's grace is poured out. But they are also detailed bill of rights. For example the ten commandments. the first one, you shall not worship any other God. it spells out the crime of idol worship. In that it also points out that God's grace and his work on the cross is sufficient to cleanse even the sin of idolatry. viewed another way God is stating that he has exclusive right to be worshiped. Let me pick another one. You shall not steal. first of all it speaks of the crime of stealing. then it points to God's grace for those who steal. At the same time it gives the right to property as stealing goes against the right to privacy. Look at do not covet. The crime is to covet for which God has grace to forgive. but do realize this points to the right to own. do not bear false witness points to right to justice. do not kill is a clear statement on the right to life. thus we have rights because God gave us human rights. God is the originator of rights. he even gave animals rights. Like the right to not boil an offspring in its mother's milk, the right of wild birds that one must not take the eggs and the mother bird. Having seen that nature does not produce equality then claiming that this artificial construct can give rights makes equality a god. And realize that the god called equality has many followers.

In Christianity many view the verse Galatians 3:27-28: *because as many of you as were immersed into Messiah in whom there is neither Jew nor Gentile, neither slave nor freeman, neither male nor female, for in union with Messiah Yeshua, you are all one*(CJB) to be the basis of all are created equal. I do believe that means when we go before God there's none with a special pass. We are all zeroes before the Alpha and Omega. But that verse in no wise says we were created in a divine factory. He is reason for rights. What he gives as rights are indeed rights up to his given limits. In Christ prejudice is discouraged. While facing God, Christ, we are all equal but when facing fellow men equity is the standard. It doesn't stop one from being a slave but in Christ the freeman is free to treat the slave like a freeman and the Jew to accept that it is God, without asking Jewry permission, betrothed from the rest of the world to himself.

Why, by the way is equality even important? Communism tried it and failed miserably. People will have unequal output thus deserving unequal rewards. Do you want same pay with someone who is slack at his job? Why do you want promotion if equality is there then there should not be any boss? In any case every struggle has its nobility. Otherwise there would be no longevity. So rights are only solidly anchored in God, all other foundations are sinking sand.

I find inequality, also called nature, to be beautiful. Let me start with a phenomenon that we are familiar with, wind. What causes the marvel of wind? It is inequality. Some places have hills, some places have valleys. Others are water, others are sand, other places forests, other places swamps others cities. No place is forever in the dark nor any forever in the light. Thus the temperature is not equal. This inequality makes the air move, and wind is formed.

It is inequality that makes us need each other. Inequality is the basis of complimentary existence. It is the DNA of interdependence. Rights exist because of God. The creator. Equal rights is communism. Right to own land in the free world means your right to own 1000 acres may seem unfair to him who only has 1/8 acre but it is justly yours. In communism all of you will have 1 acre. Even the hard working one who would have produced more and the drunkard whose 1 acre will be a bush. Needs are met because of inequality. Even the most genius mathematician needs a sweeper to keep his lab clean. And the most ingenious innovator needs mama mboga to sell him food.

Polygamy is equity and compromise. What is equity? Equity is having all needs considered. If john works hard and brings the company 50 million shillings in profits and needs ten million shillings input to produce while at the same position James brings 10 million needing two million and Arthur the one million output guy holds a demo with placards demanding to be fed the same as john because someone told him they are equal. That is what equality does. Equality, when measuring, rounds off everything to the nearest nothing. Never to the closest perfect. It pulls down great to the level of mediocre. If equality is great, why do we always equate everyone to the weakest, to the laziest, to the poorest why don't we see everyone being elevated to geniuses or millionaires or Samson? Isn't it because it is easier to reduce what exists than to increase what doesn't exist? Why don't we equate women to men standards and not just perceived male privilege thus scrap affirmative action? Men earn what they have don't they? Monogamy by force is affirmative action. It has no pillars for support other than feminism. And as Thomas Sowel said, affirmative action hurts everyone differently.

Thus I do believe it is chasing after the wind in chasing for equality. Rights are never equal though they are real. Most equalities are artificial, to our detriment.

POLYGAMY, SERVING GOD AND ANOINTING

Halleluyah! He is risen!

You know what crimson pilled me seriously? Can polygamous men and their wives serve God? In the church that you go to, can they? Or are they treated as if they are secret agents from the devil's kingdom? I know I used to treat them as such. How, then, can they call on the one they have not believed in? As it says in Rom.10.14

And how can they believe in the one of whom they have not heard? And how can they hear without someone preaching to them?(NIV)

Many believe polygamy produces jealousy and witchcraft which is not necessarily true because people with one wife also visit witch doctors. As such the nth wives and their husbands are treated like firewood for hell within church circles. Anyone who doesn't give their household to Jesus will use anything. The only service sometimes accepted from the polygamous is contributing money to congregational causes while warming the pews. So, when have you, my brother, my sister, preached a sermon targeted to the healing of these families? How do you think the healing of Jesus Christ will enter those homes? Many were a compromise alternative to divorce. Which God hates. Are you telling me that bitterness should be encouraged simply because 'he married another woman'? Does even monogamous marriage survive without God? Does the woman being the only wife make the home happier even without God? Both types need God. Both types need be watered with the word of Jesus to grow.

Even polygamists need to serve the body of Christ with their gifts and talents for spiritual growth.

Now that we have established that God is not European, cringing his nose at polygamy, how about allowing these men and women in the choir? Or in the ushering? Or helping with the Sunday schools? As much as they are totally excluded from being pastors or deacons or church elders or church committee members by the word of God they should never be treated as if we are ashamed of them. They aren't outcasts. Any Christ believing church treating polygamous families honorably with the love of Christ should be a leading church in Africa.

Did you know that at least one polygamist is mentioned serving God? Our best example of polygamous men serving God is of course David. The whole notion that people have that polygamy chases away the Holy Spirit isn't biblical. How many wives did David have when he was anointed? None? One? Answer is none. The anointing he had was real. The spirit of God was upon him. He served God both as king and as praise and worship. There are a minimum of five books related to him and his polygamous son Solomon. Was God simply giving him wife allowance for being the great faithful man after God's own heart? No. He was in God's perfect plan. Isn't it ironical that we quote the psalms and sing them while as part of the rules for praise and worship membership in many congregations it is either explicitly or silently implemented that a polygamous man or his wives apart from the first are usually not allowed to lead in singing songs from the psalms? The same psalms inspired by God through a polygamous David? Or are we intentionally blind to the fact that David and many of those priests had a few? Or is it the Old/New thing that enables us to be blind to this reality?

Isn't it true that David wouldn't be accepted as a praise and worship leader in the church today? Would even the songs he pens be sung from church to church? Would they be counted as holy inspiration? Would even Jacob be accepted as the carrier of God's promises? Solomon wouldn't even be backed by the church for candidacy as a president. And Abraham with his Hagar would never ever be considered the father of faith. They would even be labeled demoniacs.

So. First. Your other wives do not negate your salvation. Neither are they blocked from Jesus. Roman Catholic made sure Christianity was Europeanized. Every other culture was thus not judged on bible merit but on European merit. Those who came preaching Jesus unknowingly preached Europeanism with it to the detriment of local culture. Thus even you with more than one is still a child of God. Let no one yoke you with human traditions nicknamed holiness. These same Europeans and western minded preachers told my grandmother that the medical knowledge of herbs that had been passed on to her by her elders was dark magic. She died without teaching anyone! The church should apologize to Africa for robbing us of our heritage and continuity.

Secondly. Being a wife other than the first or the husband of a few doesn't mean your gifting is useless to God. Serve before God. You belong. Be an intercessor, be an usher, or like David join the choir. Encourage your family to serve. Participate in the life of the church. You are the best ambassador of Christ to polygamists like you.

Thirdly. Your knowledge of the word doesn't become corrupted like a virus infected computer just because you are a wife other than the first or the husband of a few. You know something that can teach from the word. If David did so can you.

Fourth. You are a community leader. Your gift as a community leader is a service to God. Many people use the verse about the bishop to qualify every leader chosen by Christians. I believe this is erroneous. Choosing a Member of Parliament or an MCA is not choosing a bishop. We aren't meant to turn the world into one big Monday to Monday, 24/7, church. That's an insane and unrealistic notion. The earth is real. Let's not be accused of being like the oyundi bird who came up with excuses for not helping chicken plant only to want to eat when the food was ready. The verses for choice of a king are found in Deuteronomy 17: 14-19

14 "When you come to the land that the Lord your God is giving you, and you possess it and dwell in it and then say, 'I will set a king over me, like all the nations that are around me,' you may indeed set a king over you whom the Lord your God will choose. One from among your brothers you shall set as king over you. You may not put a foreigner over you, who is not your brother. Only he must not acquire many horses for himself or cause the people to return to Egypt in order to acquire many horses, since the Lord has said to you, 'You shall never return that way again.' <u>And he shall not acquire many wives for himself,</u> lest his heart turn away, nor shall he acquire for himself excessive silver and gold. "And when he sits on the throne of his kingdom, he shall write for himself in a book a copy of this law, approved by the Levitical priests. And it shall be with him, and he shall read in *it all the days of his life, that he may learn to fear the Lord his God by keeping all the words of this law and these statutes, and doing them, that his heart may not be lifted up above his brothers, and that he may not turn aside from the commandment, either to the right hand or to the left, so that he may continue long in his kingdom, he and his children, in Israel.*

(ESV)

Electing a community leader is not electing a bishop. If it is clearly written bishop, then it is bishop. Don't oooh aaah God meant. If it is written it is written just read and apply it! What would happen if we reversed the verses for bishop and used the standards given for political leaders? Chaos! No wonder church people have horrible choices of leaders. Using the wrong standard to select leaders. You my brother are ripe for leadership. Your wives can also give a lot to society in terms of leadership and the church should be encouraged to back you up. If the verses above were used to the 2022 election instead of the verses on electing a bishop, Kenyan Christians would have elected totally different leaders.

Fifth. Be present in the affairs of the church. If given the chance to preach, preach. I wish there is a bible school that you could attend if you wanted to increase your bible knowledge without being ostracized but am not sure there's one. Maybe now there will be. Feed on the word. And be encouraged to do so remembering David and many others who were in the same position before you.

God is the father of polygamy as well as monogamy. Monogamy as well as polygamy. His bride, the church, is an amalgamation of many brides. You, me, him, her, Presbyterian, catholic, you name it. All different identities forming a unified bride.

I have come to realize that masculine chauvinism is selfish. Feminism as well is selfish. Each is a god demanding worship and sacrifice. That's why to a feminized world men are seen as toxic. Just look at the west. To a male chauvinist world feminism is toxic. Afghanistan's Taliban and Iran's religious government come to mind. And what do I mean. Taking initiative is useful selfishness. You have seen what's in it for you or for those you call your own so based on the analysis you initiate action.

Masculinity and femininity are both jealous. Marriage is the confluence, the melting pot, of many selfish goals and jealousy.

IDEAL POLYGAMY: JESUS AND THE POLYGAMOUS FAMILY

Leadership is selfish. That is why the silver-back, the lion, the mountain goat, the bull, the alpha wolf fight off competitors who try to take over. Leadership doesn't share. Masculine leadership is useful selfishness. Even Jesus died, not a moment of woke rebellion, not so that we are free from sin so as to worship anything, but to draw men unto himself. He says so himself without flattery or begging. God doesn't want to share his throne with anything. Love is positive selfishness. A man killing in war to defend his family. He wants what's best for his own. It is easier to make someone sacrifice if you can convince them that person that the sacrifice benefits them. Even God makes use of our selfishness. Jesus clearly states that there's reward in following him. Our selfishness is the hook by which the rope of reward ties us to the engine of destiny. There's a bit of selfishness in all selflessness. Leadership is being selfish enough to think you have what it takes to be listened to while being selfless enough to listen to the selfish needs of those you lead and thus direction is a confluence of positive selfishness, what we call interests or a compromise.

Masculinity's selfishness built the great world we now live in. Feminism's, not to be confused with femininity, selfishness is, in decades, destroying that work that took millennia of Masculine selfishness to build. Never forget that.

So how does selfishness become useful? Step one. Accepting who you are and accepting that these woman/women has/have done you a great honor in being your spouse(s). Don't take it for granted. It is a privilege. Don't start thinking you are a god. Don't despise them. Soft answers still break bones. How will you teach them to love one another if you aren't just? How will you abolish bitterness if you have hatred? Let's create a hypothetical case where Oliktiga has two wives; Ciku and Achuth. Achuth's view of Ciku will be shaped by what Oliktiga tells Achuth about Ciku. If Achuth is treating Ciku with open spite it's because Oliktiga has allowed it. Maybe even encouraged it.

Don't despise men you count lesser than you because though we are not created equal we are equal before God. In my tribe they really used to make fun of the man who has only one wife. When drinking the man was required to sit next to the door. They even sang songs about such a man they would sing

Ja dhako achiel, ja tingli
Ka chiemo yieng, ja tingli
Ka diend okwaro, ja tingli

Which translates to something about how the monogamist eats until he is like a goat. Which implies that even in the midst of polygamy there was monogamy.

When you cross a Rubicon bridge just remember there's no turning back. As the Luo say, you never cross a river twice. As you cross that water that you crossed has moved on. Even the slightest mention of polygamy distorts the shape of your family. Even if you turn back. For as you are turning back you will expose your back and you will have to wade against the pointed tips of your own soldiers, yes, those who risked crossing joining you in your madness, against the sharp tips of their javelins you will wade. Beyond the Rubicon lies life or death. That's why fewer and fewer cross it. Having few wives is for the few. Nobody should be forced to have none, one or few while God is okay with any of the choices.

This Rubicon is delicate and must be stepped on carefully. Do not do it like an enemy. Your first wife is not necessarily your enemy but as you cross you may make one out of her. In exodus 21:10-11 the bible, while referring to a slave married to her master, forbids her mistreatment as the existing wife when one marries another. If this is the case for a slave girl, what of a free woman? In other words adding another should be done without leaving the other. You should never be accused of abandoning the first or the second. If you cannot add without abandoning the other then don't even start.

I have heard African scholars accuse the west of practicing serial polygamy. where they marry and then divorce then marry then divorce so that one has many wives but only married to one. well, in Africa we stand accused of parallel divorce. where you marry, abandon her, add another, add her to the list of those abandoned, marry another... Christ wants you to do away with the abandonment bit. Give each of them time. Give each of them intimacy. provide for all of them. ask all of them for their opinion. Polygamy with Christ is not monogamy with un-divorced collateral.

Thus. First is prayer. Pray for all your people. Do not exclude any spouse from your prayers or any of their children. How will you have peace if you do not ask for peace from God? How will you lead that home if you do not talk to God? You are the chief priest in that home. Not the many pastors who minister to your home. Pastor is priest in church. In any case many of those pastors will only come to plant bitterness and sow discord in your home as I experienced in my childhood. You have full authority and duty from God to respectfully chase away any preacher who enters your door to preach the message of monogamy as a law and polygamy as a vice. Those wolves will only sow bitterness and hatred!

Encourage and cultivate reading of the bible. First for yourself and then for the whole family. How you lead is how they follow. Take the family to church. Lead everyone in your household to fellowship. If they are uncomfortable going to the same church or if you keep them safe distance from each other then take turns to ensure they all go to church. Lead the way in spiritual matters.

Encourage each and every member of your house to pray for each other. For decades the church has poisoned the polygamy it was supposed to heal. I grew up knowing that I should never ever pray for my stepbrothers and sisters. Never. Where did I learn that? Church! Don't you think Christ would have Catholics pray for Anglicans, Anglicans pray for Presbyterians, Presbyterians pray for Church of Holy Miracles Anointing Waters Ministry... you name it? Prayer brings unity. Even a monogamous family that doesn't encourage praying for each other is doomed to never be one.

Lead. Take initiative in the home. You have an enviable space to practice masculinity as no one woman owns you. Women in Monogamy do not view the man as a privilege but often time as a right. Those men are owned. Some only talk outside home, at home they are owned. Do not allow jealousy to breed contempt. Plan for the future of the home. Be the role model for the home. Their success is your success. Divide your time justly. Be interested in their lives and cast vision.

Love them all. It may have come from hate as you crossed the Rubicon but that doesn't mean you have to practice hatred. Take the example of Elkanah. We see him loving Hannah who by all means looks like a barren first wife. Do not despise any of your wives and do not allow any of the wives to despise another or the children to look down on each other. This also applies to the wives. Dear woman with a co-wife. That lady is not the devil. God requires you to love her. Remove all hate from your heart lest you get to heaven and be told depart from me I never knew you while you see her enter heaven. You don't know her relationship with God and bitterness can never enter heaven. You will not be excused into heaven. God is not a feminist. Start by praying for them. It will make it easier. Then when you can ensure you teach your children to pray for them.

Fifth. Be faithful to them. You shall not commit adultery still applies to you. Put a leash on your need. A woman who you haven't married is still off limits. This is also protecting the family from the effects of STIs and HIV. Even an abandoned monogamy wife will be tempted to cheat. Spend time with each one of them. Sweep each corner of their needs emotional and physical. All of them. Show each of them that they are important. Help their career growth. Be Godly. Be respectful. God expects that out of you as a man.

Work hard. Polygamy is for the strong and hard working. Provide. You have entered a territory that's hostile to the lazy dreamy simp. Feed and provide for your clan. Let the world see God even through your work. Laziness is neither Masculine nor remotely godly. When they are fed and catered for they are quiet. See all children equally. Take all children to same standard of hospital. Same standard of schools. Do not let one house in your home consider the other favored.

Ensure they know each other. There is always the funeral drama. The scourge of secret families. Maybe to avoid stigma, maybe to avoid having to face a first wife whom you find hard to challenge or correct. Maybe to avoid outright divorce. So at your funeral your other wives appear with your other children in tow. The agony this adds to agony is immeasurable. If you are going to cross this Rubicon do it as a man. Do it with strategy lest someone's daughter dies from heart attack. And with modern interactions among youth happening far from home a secret family can bring huge shame. Imagine a girl claiming your son has impregnated her only to find out the girl is your daughter? *Utajificha wapi? Utajikwamua aje?* Where will you hide? How will you wiggle out of the situation?

To you lady who is 1st, second or nth. Jesus says pray for your enemies. So pray good prayers for these people. Do not pray they be chased away. Do not pray that they be abandoned. Pray good things for them.

The other day I was asked, what would tell single ladies past thirty in the faith. I hate to say this painful truth. I do not derive any pleasure in pointing this unfortunate scenario out. Look around you in church. How many worthy single christian men do you see? How many younger ladies are available for them? Then look even closer, of those ladies you know who got married after that age where people start getting worried, how many married divorcees and widowers? Doesn't the percentage increase with age? As long as monogamy is a law it will be a fact that past some age most ladies will mainly be replacing dead and divorced women or marrying outside the church or getting married to the faulty men. I cannot recall any woman who got married after 33 who didn't replace a dead or divorced woman or got a bad deal. Do you know many?

Fathers, this is where you come in. Release your daughters to be able to be added. You hold the key. Tell your daughter it is okay for her to find family joy before she is too old to enjoy even if she is not the first one. Kindly note that if your prayers for your not so young daughters to get husbands were all to be answered your other daughters would pass away or be divorced. God provides answers, sometimes hard ones to swallow. And should it be that your daughter is the distraught first wife be there to cool down matters not pouring petrol on fire. Show her the positive side.

LAST BUT NOT LEAST

I have a strange theory about submission. Let's say you are an assistant of an assistant manager. What would you feel if you walked into the office and the watchman at the gate scoffing said "boss, *hiyo kiatu yako imeparara!*" Would you receive that criticism about your muddy or unpolished shoes kindly from someone his level? Many answer in the negative. Imagine now if the same words were used on you by the manager, how would you react? Many say they would take action. Now imagine if the president walked into your office and as he passed by your desk he looks at your shoes disapprovingly, what would be your reaction? Many I ask say they would at the slightest opportunity rush to clean it without being told. Submission is simply an outward expression of how you perceive your social value comparative to how you perceive the value of the person you are required to submit to.

Is this seen in the bible? Oh yes. I see it twice. First in 2 Samuel 6:14-23. When Michal the daughter of Sha'ul saw David dancing bible says she despised him in her heart. Look at her words. To her he became the value of a servant. Then we are told she was childless. In short there is likelihood David lost any appetite for her. Thus she remained childless. Second example is of Vashti. At some point I wondered, why was chapter 1 of Esther included in the bible? Doesn't it show lack of forgiveness? Doesn't it show God using misogyny? But something struck me here. First, feminism. Vashti threw a banquet for the women because the king Achashverosh threw one. Sound familiar? That is what feminism does. Men do something then women want to do it because men are doing it. Men develop football, women now have football. Men wrestle, now there's female wrestling if your eyes have an appetite for professional cat fights. Even to their detriment. Result? When emperor Achashverosh called her she felt she was too worthy to be paraded before men she considered of less worth. Feminism pumps up any woman's value so much that she cannot respect her man. And you know what wise people say? That where a woman's respect goes her love follows. A man however can do what a man must do for his woman even the one he does not respect as long he owns her. As a result of the lack of submission and subsequent disrespect the king added a whole harem of wives.

There's nothing that kills a man's desire for a woman than a woman who sees her value as high heaven. The type who see themselves as having so much value that as some put it, you are supposed to kiss the ground on which they walk on. Such feminist ideals only make her see rugs in men. These are women who require, not affirmation, but adoration from men, divas with such high value that they exact worship from men. Worship in words, money and presence. Such overvalued women require you to tell them the words you tell God more times than you tell God, require your money to the extent of owning you, you will even spend the tithe on their demands, your presence too where they want you to be and such are disturbed when you indicate you don't think of them all the time.

You cannot own such a woman. She owns herself. You can only rent her at great servitude until you end up feeling worthless. I saw on twitter one time of a woman who had a to-do list indicating what each activity convinces her to concede. Of course top prize was sex. If your man has to wash dishes to earn a kiss, frequently tell you I love you in front of everyone to see you briefly without clothes, somersault and hop on one leg to choose the style then dear lady does he own you? Even if you emulate the famed Ugandan *nyabbo* ways of expressing submission kneeling to their *ssebos* your overvaluation of self will show up and with your own hands, as Proverbs 14; 1 says, you will destroy your house. That's how important it is. Ask the men and you will realize that that's one way many polygamies, permitted by God, starts. Because the man has a woman at home who believes she is worth 10 times her weight in gold and her man is just a rug.

The best marriage in my view is between a man who owns his woman, not as property but as his wife and a wife doesn't consider being owned as demeaning and is not scared. Modern society has tried to retrain men so that they discard the art of owning their women. At the same time reprogramming women so that they are attached to a man but not owned. Hence the birth of simping madness like open marriages. Just check any wild animal documentary and you will see how the males own their females. If you can convince a man that he will own something he will go for it. That's how a ruler convinces his men to attack another country. The promise of owning lands and gold and even taking their women has always been a motivator of aggression. Only a useless man will die for a woman he does not own. You only fence what you own or what you have rented. Boundaries. Fools worship their women in the name of chivalry instead of owning them. As Fela Kuti rightly sang, "*lady na master. Lady no woman.*" The amount of affection and oneness a man shows is directly proportional to how much he owns you dear lady or how much he thinks he owns you. Forget what feminism teaches, men are still animals within and the minute he perceives he doesn't own you the gentleman side of him flies out of the window. It is a natural reaction. Even mad men in their madness have something they perceive they own. One lady once told me, "these are modern times, men must change," well unfortunately men only change what is not working. Come to think of it, when a man pays a prostitute or sponsors a side chick, some are just guaranteeing the ownership they cannot get at home. Men enjoy submission and ownership. Ownership, the feeling of "she is mine and I make the rules" or "it is mine" is why real men enjoy earning something more than undeservedly being given.

Dear man younger than myself. Listen to what I am telling my younger self. Manning up when you are married is difficult. You have seen many men go for masculinity teaching or training and their marriage suffers. My theory is that by that time you have a woman by your side who loves the simp in you. Allow me to call these feminists SiLoWo, Simp Loving Women. The simp you are at that time attracted a feminist woman who /wants to lead. The ones who cannot be owned. Then suddenly you want to take charge. There will be obvious clashes. Women don't let go what they get. She is driving and you will have to wrestle the steering wheel from her. Fireworks. I have come to the realization that men characterized as 'bad boys' tend to get a better bargain in a relationships and marriage as compared to the 'your wish is my command oh queen' type of man. Man up young. Then the one you catch will be attracted to your masculinity.

And what is manning up? It starts with setting clear manly boundaries. Knowing what will not work for you and sticking to it uncompromisingly. Unfortunately standards come with experience. And that's bad news because many times men end up gaining experience on the job. Learning from other's failures is way more cost effective and quicker. When they say experience is the best teacher they mostly mean failure is a good teacher. Until recent times it was politically incorrect to pass masculine standards of old. Knowing what you want and what you will accept is freedom and never compromise. Learn from those who failed before you. And if you are older do not listen to women saying "don't say anything or else..." that is how the previous generation of men failed the current. They allowed feminism to tell the story of masculinity. Manning up is taking charge. Honing your decision making skills and cultivating the ability to take initiative is paramount for personal and professional growth. It's better to make bad decisions than hide very safe behind your wife. Learning from other men makes the learning curve shorter.

Be cautious about becoming the type of man defined by most westernized churches. Many churches get active initiative driven great men and turn them into passive good men.

That brand of masculinity is infected with feminism. You hear comments in simp approving church circles like "*nyumba inaendeleanga ni ile bwana amekaliwa*"- literally a good house is one where the husband has been sat on. In short where the wife has both initiative and takes charge. You hear phrases like "happy wife happy life." In short what a man does is duty and anything women do is sacrifice and women are never wrong. This is the type of masculinity I have heard being preached so many times! Avoid being that man the way you avoided COVID. That is a weak man. Even good women are poisoned by men without boundaries. Most preachers encourage bible boundaries but by preaching that husbands are to become wife pleasers and men to become women pleasers they negate the same bible boundaries. You cannot please and enforce boundaries at the same time. Being a nice guy is building on a failed feminized masculinity foundation.

You hear people speaking of how not following the wife's decision led to a loss. Thus it is common to hear in church someone extolling how a man is supposed to pick the wife's decision by default. That is the process through which a man abdicates his decision making role. The old method of listen to her input but make your decision or better still have your decision and refine it with her input still works. The only route to a man making good decisions is through the lessons of bad decisions. If you keep disguising your wife's decision as yours who is actually in charge? You or her? You hear many ladies saying church men are boring. I believe this refers to a man who has been trained into a nice pet of a man. A man who gets a wife just to be led by the wife. The last great initiative he takes is proposing to her. She tests your standards and you bend them to accommodate her whims. She makes decisions for you and you allow her to take charge. Instead of asking for opinion you ask for permission. It is tragic that many church circles encourage your sacrificing yourself as a man more than taking charge including sacrificing your initiative on the altar of feminism. There is a word "simping" that fits this.

Even Jesus was not a nice guy. That didn't make him evil. He is righteousness itself. He is God, only God is good, he is good. However even in his righteousness he still has boundaries and he whipped money launders and overturned the tables of those who dared cross his boundaries. Jesus did not start wars so as to conquer but he did conquer. Christian men should be as harmless, innocent, inoffensive as doves and as shrewd as snakes. Purposefully hostile not intentionally. Like Jesus knowing when to be a lamb and when to be lion. Masculinity is not necessarily about being rude and rough but knowing what is needed and standing firm. One can be firm without being rude.

Guard your masculinity.

GIGO. Garbage in garbage out. One source of betatisation is love ballads. They are a heap of gynocentric lyrics that revolve around how a man should, must find and is helpless without a woman to worship. You will be a warrior defeated before any battle. It's easy to dismiss them as mere music until long after you have conceded boundaries. Constantly feeding your subconsciousness with diva worship is one way to make your boundaries wobbly. Take care what music you listen to.

I once told myself that for a whole week I will not speak to those men I call friends who are my friends because I married their friend or because they are the husband of my wife's friend. I was shocked. I spoke to no one. It hit me that I was surrounded by men whose connection to me is my wife. I realized that if I disagreed with my wife I shall have no man to stand with me. Never allow yourself to be in that situation. Men who are around you because of your wife will not help grow you as a man. They are your male 'feminine' friends. Your interaction with them is peppered with feminine censorship. You cannot be open with them and tell them you have issues with their friend. Some of them might even be hanging around hoping you fail and they take over.

That brings me to the next point. *Thou shalt not covet.* Exodus 20:17

This is easily the most forgotten commandment. Indeed modern society has normalized covetousness, even extolled from pulpits. Yet in my experience it comes down to something very simple. If it has an owner, and you desire it, if it is something that can be bought offer a price. If the owner doesn't want to sell it move on. Where you can buy it, by all means go on and buy it. In many instances where there's a clear owner, a husband: we tend to respect that.

Problem is the grey area. Where we can convince ourselves that someone doesn't own enough or doesn't own at all or as some people coumaflage it, we claim by faith. Those misleading preachings of possessing vineyards you didn't plant, houses you didn't build. Please note Israel was being paid for being God's tool for punishing the Canaanites. They were not just being given. They earned it. You meet some delusional brethren walking around claiming people's cars walking around calling people's houses theirs, looking at people's fiancés and muttering "my wife" under their breathe. Repent! Let me use real examples that I have actually seen. Someone is buying land and has signed an agreement. You want it. You use more money to dislodge that agreement and the other buyer's deposit is refunded. You haven't stolen it right? Legitimate deal, right? Aren't you telling yourself, "nothing personal, just business?" But are you sure that someone is not walking away feeling robbed of ownership of a good deal? Aren't you the cause of an agreement broken somewhere? Brother, repent that covetousness.

Or the example of workers. We say it is a free market. Right? Oh yes we convince ourselves that no one belongs to anyone in today's world. Let us say Benjamin is Odhoch's worker. Brings in a tidy two million gross per month to that business. If only Benjamin was working for me. So I offer him a high retainer, a high salary, flexible working hours, the works. Problem is that by the time my covetousness wins over Benjamin I am not getting the same loyal employee he was. He now crosses over as one who has learnt that disloyalty pays and I taught him. He has tasted the fruit of disloyalty. I will forever struggle to be the highest bidder. That is how I watched covetousness ruin my investment. That's how you can be having the best workers but because you got them through covetousness they bring you down.

What of relationships? Here we get the most subtle of grey areas. Dating. We are in the 21st century, they say no man owns a woman. Right? You might want to rethink that. Men protect what they own. Men relate by owning. Even when supporting a football team men convince themselves that they own the team they are cheering thus the team deserves their loyalty. Just listen to the language. "*Sisi tutawapiga 10-0.*" The language is full of ownership. Dear feminist if he doesn't own you he won't provide for you, protect you and give you babies. He is your man when he owns you. That is how women with no beauty and no education and no money and no diva trappings manage to keep high value men glued to them. It is easier for them to make the men feel like they own them. The day he realizes how much less he owns the less his ownership behaviors will be.

That is guaranteed. But please note, feminists own men. Just watch divorce courts and you will see how.

To many people, if she is not yet married she is available. So you decide to outdo the boyfriend in the story whom in your view doesn't own her enough. My friend. That is one battle you should be happy to lose. Why? Which is the biggest boundary between a man and his woman? You are seeing her and she is not seeing another? Now the shoe will be on the other foot. As you take her on a date behind another man's back what you are in essence implying is that you don't mind being with her while she has another man. As you buy someone's girlfriend gifts please remember you are telling her you don't mind her receiving gifts from men when she is yours. Someone's girlfriend is as good as his wife because she might as well become. You will never fully win her over. You won a battle of comparison. What assures you she will not compare in future. There will always be something where the other guy was better. Worse still what did you have to relinquish to make yourself the better offer? A wise friend of mine once told me things don't just go wrong, they start wrong.

Starting courtship with covetousness is like building a house using good stones but the wrong mortar mixture. Rich Cooper talks of betatisation by a thousand concessions. Covetousness starts off courtship with major concessions. And here is the key that I learnt; whatever you get through the fruit of covetousness ends up owning you. Ask Ahab. Naboth's plot ended up owning him, defining his legacy and the rest of his life. Dogs drank his blood and his wife ended up eaten by dogs. Just because of coveting a piece of land. You may out-buy or out-deal someone most likely to realise you didn't need the property or end up with a loan higher than you intended. Free market it is but that worker will own your profits. What did you do to convince the girl, money? She will come for it like the Babylonians went for the gold Hezekiah showed off. Is it brains? Is it physique? Is it freedom? There's an aspect of you enticing her to leave what she has and come over not just to enjoy the man you are but to own that man. Covetousness courtship makes you see the woman of your desire as a woman you cannot live without. It blinds you.

Yet a man should look for the woman he can live with not one he cannot live without. I have learnt that until you can live without that girl you love life with her will be a betatisation process. This is best enforced before marriage. You must have boundaries that either she follows or you are willing to cut her lose. They say love is blind marriage is the eye opener but i warn you that boundaries are the best eye opener. They will keep you from learning you can live without her when there are children and in-laws to handle. Wisen your boundaries by learning from the failures of other men.

Any woman who can allow you to court her, to be her spare man, while she has accepted another courtship is faulty. She is the type that owns herself such that you cannot own her. She will be attached to you but there's a depth of oneness you won't get. Even if you get her she will be like a student on attachment, a company cannot count that student as permanent and pensionable. If someone's girlfriend is enjoying your attention here is my unsolicited advice; RUN FOR DEAR LIFE!

Learn to take charge without being rude or offensive. As I have told you, masculinity is useful selfishness. You do not have to be rude or conceited or high handed to be a man. I have learnt there's power in listening. Loving that girl or if you have more than one then girls means you listen to their needs. Be like Jesus. Being all powerful yet he still listens to us. Even our dumb prayers and those things we cannot even tell our women. Remember the example of Rehoboam? After being crowned king the people sent Jeroboam to tell him not to be a dictator like Solomon. He consulted. The old wise men told him to relent. His age mates told him to tell the people "my father's waist is a big as my little finger. Where he used whips I will use scorpions." What did that lead to? A split into the northern and Southern Kingdoms. Being a man doesn't mean harshly treating women.

Of course after being red pilled after being the perfect nice guy one is highly likely to be harsh to women. There's that self-hate at the feminized man one has become that one violently pulls away from and regrets and confusion. To be pulled into a haka moment. When the man in you is awakened better spend time alone so that you don't expose your family to Spartan war cries and Maori *Ka mate* chants and *Jowi jamwomo*! Nothing new, our fore fathers were there.

There is a story I was told from the Rendille people. One day an elephant attacked a village. The chief ran away. The head warrior ran away. His deputies ran away. The elephant was causing havoc in the village. Suddenly a man jumped into the middle of the village and speared the mammoth to death. The horrified villagers got out of their houses one by one.

One woman, so awed by the feat shouted, "Who is the brave man who killed this elephant? I must have his child".

The bewildered villagers told her, "It is your husband".

Shocked, she retorted, "You are lying. That coward cannot kill a fly."

Again the villagers told her, "It is your husband".

Her response, much to the villagers' dismay was, "Nkt! Then this elephant is nothing but a mosquito if that man can kill it."

Ever been a simp? The story is an accurate illustration of African wisdom that once a woman sees you a simp you will be a simp to her no matter how you change for the better. Realizing that God did not create you to beg and grovel for the sake of intimacy can make you a "bad man". Just by drying up the begging, groveling and woman worship you will automatically have become bad. Having your eyes opened and you look back and see you are the best second fiddle, her reasonable choice being led by her and not her best choice leading her can be devastating` and intimacy killing. Knowing that your woman having many rules, dos and don't, for you might be symptomatic of loving you with her brains not her heart, not being inherently liked, can really sober you up. That place of realization that nagging actually stems from a lack of respect and respect is founded on how much social value she sees in you can be heartbreaking. I have learnt that reclaiming masculinity by being tough without being rough is a tricky juggle.

Starting to have standards and sticking by them is hard work. It is much easier to slip back to letting everyone have their way at your expense. Let God help you govern your household without violence. Practice taking charge and taking initiative. Never let your leadership be weakened by accepting the 'woke' world view that men are inherently dumb and a decision is good just because it was made by a woman. When you make a mistake it doesn't mean you should say yes to all your woman says and camouflage it as your decision. You will make no mistakes but you will go nowhere. How long will you hide beneath your wife's skirt? You need to rise and lead not be a puppet king like the last khans of the Ilkhanate and the golden horde. You need to rule not her ruling through you. Mistakes are only losses when they don't teach you. Mistakes are the food for greatness. Make mistakes, learning to handle mistakes is necessary for leadership. Through mistakes one learns to make better decisions. Listen to her or them and make your decision. Like our fathers did. The beauty of polygamy is that no one woman owns that man.

Are you a church leader? I believe there's a chance to improve the Marriage Act. There should be introduced the category of Afro-Christian marriage. What has always been referred to as Christian marriage is actually Roman Christian marriage. It was Christianity bent to Roman culture. Why must you pastor insist on *conferatio*? Even the ring and the white dress were all roman tradition. That places roman culture above our cultures. Now let's bend it to African culture. Go and bless couples in their African weddings. Let them exchange vows in their parents homes church and white wedding is not a must!

This opens up another legal aspect. I ask myself, before the coming of the white man, which was the legally recognized wedding venue? The bride's father's homestead, wasn't it? And who were the accepted officials? Her father and her clan representatives, isn't it? the current laws on venue and officials supplanted that African norm which is accepted in the bible.

I propose we undo this insult to African custom by declaring a bride's parent's home as a wedding venue so that a certificate issued will be valid. In this case that certificate should be the one called marriage certificate. Also clan elders can be authorized wedding officials. They used to be before this *mzungu* system usurped their roles. This way our collective mindset will be africanised as *nyombo, posa, koito, ruracio* and so on replace roman tradition church wedding.

Further to these as a way of accepting that instead of divorce, one may add another wife and they stay together, I propose a clause allowing change from Christian marriage to African Christian marriage. We have laws for changing land from residential to commercial. There should be a way of change of user. In this a commutation payment must be paid and a well-structured process needs to be created. The first wife's status as a wife ahead of the others must be guaranteed by the man and equitable provision for children must also be guaranteed and spelled out in the process. Christians have to decide which process is evil and ungodly, divorce or polygamy.

As ambassadors of Christ I do believe even in evangelism we need to sieve out the roman culture from what we preach. If we evangelize to a Muslim with four wives what shall we tell him? That Christ wants him to divorce his wives? This is how this Romanization affects even evangelism. It is easy to trot the globe believing your inherited European values make sense and represent the zenith of civilization and people will just hear and accept them. There's a whole world out there of Muslim polygamists and African polygamists waiting to be preached to about Christ and they have their own culture, parts of which God approves, they don't need Roman culture along with Christianity.

I also believe we need African minded Christians to do scientific research on polygamy. I mean, if man is not the innovator of polygamy, if it came from God, then it must have some good. God doesn't give bad things to his own. We have to search for his wisdom in it. How did he want it to be? Maybe it accounts for the declining populations of countries where polygamy is a crime. Maybe the excess number of women not owned is manure for feminism as they rationalize singleness as a coping mechanism and disparage motherhood. Questions like does Christianity indeed help polygamous homes? Are there women who would prefer to share in a Christ centered neo African setup? Where there's good polygamy, what are the benefits to the women and the men? I mean, if God in his wisdom owns an idea then it must have positives. One area of research is case studies of good polygamy. Another question is how does work and liberty affect women sexually? Have appetites changed over the years? Also what is the effect of coerced coitus on the persons and their relationship? The issue with negative labels is that it becomes politically incorrect to view such an issue as positive. A proper balanced researched documentation in a publicly consumable form is needed.

In conclusion. Am not a marriage expert. I hold no expertise in philosophy. I am not even a sociology expert. I just observe. So if you find this info useful use it. One of the early missioners to East Africa said that the crown had the duty to spread the following three Cs; Christianity, Commerce and Civilization. In short to them we weren't human enough. They came to replace not to improve. We shouldn't view ourselves as foreigners view us. Christianity does not imply westernization! I dream of seeing Afro-Christians!

About the Author